DISCOVERING
God

A Study for Learning about God and
Growing Closer to Him

Hermie Reynolds

Discovering God
Copyright © 2013 by Hermie Reynolds

All rights reserved. No part of this book may be reproduced, stored in a retrieval system, or transmitted in any form or by any means-electronic, mechanical, photocopy, recording, or otherwise-without prior written permission of the copyright owner, except by a reviewer who wishes to quote brief passages in connection with a review for inclusion in a magazine, website, newspaper, podcast, or broadcast. Cover imagery © James Thew - Fotolia.com.

All Scripture quotations, unless otherwise indicated, are taken from the *New King James Version*®. Copyright © 1982 by Thomas Nelson, Inc. Used by permission. All rights reserved.

Scripture quotations marked AMP are taken from the *Amplified® Bible*, Copyright © 1954, 1958, 1962, 1964, 1965, 1987 by The Lockman Foundation. Used by permission." (www.Lockman.org)

Scripture quotations marked NLT are taken from the Holy Bible, *New Living Translation*, copyright 1996, 2004. Used by permission of Tyndale House Publishers, Inc., Wheaton, Illinois 60189. All rights reserved.

Scripture marked MSG or The Message are taken from *The Message*. Copyright © 1993, 1994, 1995, 1996, 2000, 2001, 2002. Used by permission of NavPress Publishing Group.

ISBN: 978-0-9981529-0-5

Dedication

My heart is filled with gratitude toward my heavenly Father, His Son, Jesus, and my companion, the Holy Spirit. I know that without God's involvement in my life, this book would not have come about. The glory of the finished product belongs to God.

Thank you to my wonderful husband, John, and my children, Luke, Janien, Xander, Estian, and Morgan, who have supported and encouraged me to pursue what God has placed in my heart. Thank you to my mom who has always been an encouragement to me.

Thank you for your prayers, friendship, and help, Margie and Janeen. Thank you to all my wonderful friends who prayed for me to make all this possible; there are simply too many to name who have encouraged me and been a support to our family.

Endorsements

"*Discovering God* is a good teaching on who God is. It is written in an easy-to-read conversational style, as Hermie shares her own life along with probing questions and answers from Scripture. This book is a great source for new Christians who are looking for a well-rounded teaching about God. This would be a wonderful tool for small discipleship groups."

Sandy Warner
www.thequickenedword.com

"*Discovering God* is a wonderful resource for both new and seasoned believers; teens and adults alike. A gifted teacher, Hermie Reynolds invites us on a treasure hunt to discover who God is. She makes complicated theological concepts—immanence, transcendence, eternity, the Trinity, sovereignty, free will, sanctification, and justification—accessible by painting word pictures from everyday life. Each chapter is chock-full of gems: Scripture, quotes, and examples from her own life. Thought-provoking questions at the end of each chapter encourage us to dig deep for treasure; to ask the big questions—Who is God? What is He like? Does He care about me? These are not fill-in-the-blank questions, but questions that draw us from head to heart; to a bone-deep knowledge of how much God loves us, why He sent Jesus to save us, and how the Holy Spirit makes His home within us when we give our lives to Jesus. A life-changing treasure awaits you within the pages of this study."

Kathleen Deyer Bolduc
Author of *Autism & Alleluias*

"Out of years of pursuing God through prayer, worship, and diligent study of the Word of God, Hermie has crafted from her experience a tool for the individual and/or group to grow in and troll the very depths of the vast expanse of God's greatness. From one who has personally prayed with and watched Hermie live her life before the Lord in the prayer room I am confident you will find this material to be rich in the spirit of wisdom and revelation of our God. As you read this book may the witness of the Holy Spirit in you give testimony to the qualities and nature of our glorious Father."

Walter P. Barr
Director & Lead Pastor of the Cincinnati House of Prayer (C-HOP)

"Hermie's teaching style is Spirit-filled, personable, and engaging to children, youth, and adults. This face-to-face teaching style is captured in Hermie's writing as well, drawing readers into the pages, encouraging them in their quest to know more about God and an intimate relationship with Him. Hermie has bathed her writing in constant prayer and set herself before the Lord every step of the way. In so doing, I believe her words will speak to the hearts of many, and I strongly recommend its reading. It is my hope and prayer that the Lord would use this wonderful tool to bring some to a saving knowledge of Jesus and others to a deeper revelation of His love, to the praise and glory of God."

John Gordon
Associate Director and Pastor, Cincinnati House of Prayer

Contents

Foreword	9
Introduction	11
How to Use This Book for Group Discussion	15
Chapter 1: Meeting the Most Important Person in the Universe	17
Chapter 2: God, Everywhere Present in the Universe	25
Chapter 3: Powerful, Majestic God	33
Chapter 4: Is God a Person?	43
Chapter 5: God Is Not Limited by Time	53
Chapter 6: All Powerful, Sovereign God	63
Chapter 7: God Created Me	73
Chapter 8: God Gives Me a Choice	81
Chapter 9: A Joyful, Loving, Tenderhearted, Kind Father	93
Chapter 10: God Keeps His Promises	105
Chapter 11: God Is Light and There Is No Darkness in Him	115
Chapter 12: God Is Love	125
God's Invitation	135

Foreword

Our view of God defines who we are, so it stands to reason that the goal of life ought to be the study of God Himself. This has been one of the expressed goals of the Cincinnati House of Prayer since its beginning. Not surprising, many who seek such a life find themselves in the prayer room.

I first met Hermie in the context of prayer. I've met many who consider themselves "a praying person," but far fewer who actually give themselves to the ministry of intercession. Hermie is definitely the latter. It's from a deep place of intimacy with Jesus that a framework was built for what has now become this book.

You can often learn quite a bit about a person when you hear them pray. I remember the tenor and quality of Hermie's prayers over the years, how often the overflow of her heart spilled forth with the knowledge of God. This gave me reason to like this little South African lady with the wonderful accent.

I'm continually impressed with her entire family, all hardworking lovers of God, each with their own unique calling in God and pursuing it wholeheartedly. I've heard it said that, "we teach what we know, but we reproduce who we are." Perhaps there is no clearer example of that truth than in our own family, and reproduced in the Reynolds family is a quality, a love, and a strength that I've seen in very few.

Over the years Hermie has written and taught various classes, but I think her favorite preparation has been contemplating the attributes of God. The many people who have taken her classes and pored over this material have encouraged her in drafting this book.

Discovering God

If you have a desire to know God, to discover what He is like—what He thinks and feels—then this book may be for you. Why not give yourself to staring at God, and see what He produces in your life? This book will help you do just that.

Rusty Geverdt
Founder of Cincinnati House of Prayer

Introduction

Who is God? What is He like? Does He care about me? Those are questions many people ask themselves. We learn about God in the Bible; still many Christians find it hard to connect with Him. God is Spirit (John 4:24) and that is one reason why it is hard for us to understand Him. How do we connect with God if we can't feel Him or touch Him? My prayer is that this book will help you to understand God better and teach you how to connect with Him. The Bible was used as the foundation to learn about the character of God and enriched with examples, stories, and quotes to bring greater understanding. Enjoy the journey to discover the God who not only created the universe, but also created you. He holds the universe together, but He is also intricately involved in all the details of your life.

Daniel 11:32b tells us, "The people who know their God shall be strong, and carry out *great exploits*." Knowing who God is and what His character is like will build our faith and trust in Him. It will protect us from being swayed from our faith and will cause us to take a strong, unwavering stand for Him.

Growing up I had a desire to have a relationship with God. Our family attended church every Sunday. For me it felt like God was up there in heaven and I was down here on earth and I wasn't sure if He really cared about me. At age 23, I attended a Bible study and learned that I needed to surrender my life to Jesus.

Following Jesus was the best decision I have made in my life. It brought me into a personal relationship with God through His Son, Jesus Christ. Not long after this decision, I met my husband. We got married and we were blessed with four beautiful children and a wonderful son-in-law.

Discovering God

The decision to follow Jesus didn't guarantee me a life without troubles. Looking back, I can see God has helped me through all the difficulties I encountered along the way. I have His Holy Spirit who lives in me and who is with me and leads and helps me wherever I go.

This book came forth in the process of raising our own four children, and seeing the challenges they faced. There was a time when I was very concerned about our youngest son who was drawn into electronic games. Although we set limits, I was concerned that it was hindering his spiritual growth. One morning I woke up from a very short, strange dream. My son was in the dream, and a voice said, "Not wormwood"; instead the name of a person was mentioned. I didn't know who this person was and asked my children if they knew someone with that name. My daughter answered, "Mom, we're attending a young adult conference in two weeks and that man is one of the main speakers." God had my attention. Researching wormwood, I read it was a bitter plant. It felt like wormwood represented the things that were pulling my son away from God. I was invited to chaperone the group of young people to the conference and was curious to find out what this speaker had that could counteract the wormwood, or bad influences, that pull my children away from their commitment to Jesus. Soon I discovered this man was the director of a Bible school and he was known for the Christology class that he taught. Hmm, I thought, it made sense; if young people really know Jesus and have a strong relationship with Him, they will make better choices.

Searching the bookstore before we left the conference, I found two books about the attributes of God. Not long after we arrived home, I received the opportunity to teach a youth group. My own boys were in that group and I decided to teach them about the attributes of God, eventually teaching about Jesus, and then about the Holy Spirit. The young ones grew stronger in their faith and I saw how helpful it was to have a strong foundation in our belief in God.

Eventually I became more involved in the House of Prayer in our city. I was given the opportunity to develop a six-week class about the attributes of God. Three years later, I received a prophecy about writing a book. I never thought that I could be a writer; but encouraged by the word, I started to write this book.

Hermie Reynolds

The studying and teaching that I have done about the attributes of God helped me to be able to write this book. It has been a faith-building and enriching journey for me. Studying the attributes of God made me realize that I didn't know God as well as I thought I did. It has strengthened my faith and the faith of others who took the class. May it build and strengthen your faith in God too.

This is my prayer for you: May God reveal Himself to you as you read through this book. May you grow deeper in your faith, trust, and relationship with Him. May you come to know His wonderful love and how faithful He is to those who put their trust in Him.

How to Use This Book for Group Discussion

This book can be read by itself or it can be used as small group material. When used for a small group, read the chapter that will be discussed ahead of time. If you have questions or thoughts about a section, mark it and talk about it in your group. Here are some ideas for how you can structure your group time and some basic guidelines you may want to set for your group to help keep things orderly.

Ideas for Group Time (One hour long)

- Welcome everyone and open with prayer.

- Use the first fifteen minutes to share questions or thoughts people had about the chapter. If someone has many questions and the leader feels it will take all the group time to answer it, then schedule a different time to talk about it, unless you can put a time limit on the discussion and it will benefit the whole group. Keep in mind that some of the questions people have in earlier chapters might be answered in later chapters.

- Use the next fifteen to twenty minutes for discussion questions. The questions are focused on digging deeper into Scripture and applying what each person is learning about God in their own lives. The questions don't have to be answered ahead of time; that can be done in the group.

- Use the remaining time for prayer and personal ministry. If the group is big enough and there are Christians who know how to pray for others, then divide the group in smaller groups of two or three people to pray. If the group is less than ten people, the person who wants to receive prayer can be seated in the middle while the others in the group pray for them. Often with this kind of prayer, the Holy Spirit will give different people impressions or pictures or prayers to pray that are very specific and helpful to the person being prayed for.

Set Some Guidelines for Discussion

- Don't get into any argumentative discussions. Discussions about creation vs. evolution, etc. could just lead the whole group time off track; these arguments could take up all the time and nothing would get accomplished. If questions like that come up, schedule a different time to talk about it or recommend a good book. Be sensitive to what the Holy Spirit wants to do, and pull the group back if the discussion goes in an argumentative direction. The purpose of the study is getting to know God and talking about how He wants to meet us in my everyday life. Stay to the topic.

- Don't rush through the Scriptures; ask the Holy Spirit what He wants to speak to each of you as you go through the Scriptures and discuss them. The questions also have practical life application.

- The leader of the group should decide how to minister to those who need prayer.

Chapter 1: Meeting the Most Important Person in the Universe

"As the deer pants for the water brooks, so pants my soul for You, O God" (Psalm 42:1).

People have struggled through the ages to come to an understanding of who God is. The Bible gives us information about God's character. God has created us for more than just having a lot of knowledge about Him. He also longs to have a relationship with us. Relationships have their struggles, and that is what is perplexing to many people. How do I get to know God and have a relationship with Him when I can't see Him?

The apostle Paul had a lot of knowledge about God and he zealously tried to obey God. In his zeal, he even captured Christians and caused them to be put to death. Paul was alive when Jesus walked the earth. He was a devout Pharisee (Acts 23:6) and was against Jesus. After the death of Jesus, Paul persecuted Christians. An encounter with Jesus brought him to a radical turnaround in which he became a Christian (Acts 9:1-7). The Bible tells us that Jesus is the only way to God (John 14:6). Paul came to know that truth: that Jesus was the Son of God, the Messiah, sent to the earth to pay for sins and to restore mankind back into a relationship with God (John 3:16).

Meeting Jesus radically changed Paul's life and his walk with God. I am sure that after Paul came to the belief that Jesus was the Messiah, he thought, *Jesus walked the earth; I could have known Him personally while He was on earth, but I didn't*. Paul was in the same position that we are in today. Jesus is not walking the earth anymore, yet He is alive and we can get to know Him as we read the Bible and walk in a personal relationship with Him. Paul's desire is beautifully described in the Amplified Bible: "[For my determined purpose is] that I may know Him [that I may progressively become more deeply and intimately acquainted with Him, perceiving and recognizing and understanding the wonders of His Person more strongly and more clearly]" (Philippians 3:10a).

Paul came a long way; from causing the death of Christians to a man with an intense desire to know God. No matter what you have done in life, you can have the same turnaround and come to know God in a deep and personal way.

Learning God's Language

Growing in our relationship with God is like learning a foreign language. God speaks "Spirit" language and at first we do not know His language. We read in the Bible how He worked in people's lives and helped them. Some of it was supernatural; for example, we read of angels showing up and people having dreams. Jesus demonstrated God's power in His ministry. We also find practical wisdom in the Bible. We need to embrace both. Practical wisdom gives us a good foundation to produce good fruit, from where we can grow more in the gifts and power of the Holy Spirit.

God, My Hero

A good book has a hero in it. He is strong and risks his life to rescue a princess or fight for a cause. He faces danger and death for something or someone he feels is worth the conquest. Daniel wrote, "The people who know their God shall be strong, and carry out great exploits" (Daniel 11:32b). Would you like to be one who accomplishes great things for God? First you need to know the one for whom you are doing this. Is He worthy of receiving all your love, all your attention, all your affection? Yes, indeed, He is! Remember, we will not lay down our lives for someone we don't know.

Meeting the President of a Country

How would I go about meeting and getting to know the president of a country? I would read news articles about him, click "Like" on his facebook page, or read his biography. The best option would be if my dad were a friend of the president and our family visited with his family from time to time. Then I could get close to him. I could see what he likes to eat and read, and how he spends his time. This would show me what is important to him.

It is the same with God. We need to get to know Him. He reveals Himself through Jesus who came to earth. We can identify and understand Jesus more easily, because He was a man who walked the earth. We can learn about God from the Bible, Christian books, and other Christians. Trying to get to know God just from outside sources is like only reading about the President. We come to God through His Son, Jesus. Jesus opened the door for us to get access to God (Colossians 1:21-22, Hebrews 10:19). When Jesus left the earth, He said He will give us the Holy Spirit to help us (John 14:26). When we get to know God through Jesus and yield to the leading of His Holy Spirit, we get to know Him personally. "Book knowledge" is important and we learn a lot from the Bible, books, and other people. But the most valuable lessons we learn are those we learn as we personally follow the example of Jesus and the leading of the Holy Spirit in every area of our lives.

God is the most important person we will ever meet and come to know. He has given each person an eternal spirit, which is inside of our bodies and which we cannot see. The Bible tells us that God has created us, body (the physical body), soul (mind, will, and emotions), and spirit. "May your whole spirit, soul, and body be preserved blameless at the coming of our Lord Jesus Christ" (1 Thessalonians 5:23b). My personal human spirit given to me by God will live forever. The day that I breathe out my last breath, my spirit and soul will return to God. It is of the utmost importance to know where I will spend eternity, and to know the one with whom I am going to spend it.

God, the Creator of the Universe

The first introduction to God is as the Creator of the Universe. When we create something, we need paint and paper or some kind of material to make it. We cannot create something from nothing. We read in Genesis 1 several times where God spoke and the earth, plants, and animals were created. "Then God said, 'Let there be light'; and there was light"

(Genesis 1:3). Every time God created, He spoke. The word *said* in Genesis 1 is a verb. It means: "said, speak, decree, an order, a weighty command."[1] God said, He spoke, He gave a command and night and day started, the waters separated and dry ground was formed, the grass, trees, and animals were created. What authority is in His voice! He can speak and create.

We can influence people with what we say. We have seen that in politics in the way a great speech can sway people to believe something. A speaker at a training I attended one time shared how she walked into a restaurant and there was an old piano in the room; she made the remark that the piano looked like it could fall apart at any time. Very soon after that, the piano fell over. The Holy Spirit spoke to her and said that she had wanted God to anoint her words, and He had; but when God does that, He anoints the positive and negative words we speak. It doesn't just work for the positive ones. God wants to give us power to speak forth His kingdom on earth. If you want anointing and power on the words you speak, you need to be careful with the words you speak.

God reveals Himself as one God, three Persons. In John 1 we read that Jesus was present at creation. Jesus is the living Word (John 1:1-3). We can read a play; but when actors come and make the play alive, we can see and experience it. That is what happened with the earth. God spoke and Jesus and the Holy Spirit brought creation alive. It is important to know that the triune God—Father, Son, and Holy Spirit—were present before the creation of the earth. We read about Jesus being born as a baby, but Jesus existed before the foundation of the world (Revelation 13:8).

We meet Jesus in Genesis as the Word. "In the beginning was the Word, and the Word was with God, and the Word was God. He was in the beginning with God. All things were made through Him, and without Him nothing was made that was made" (John 1:1-3). In God's timing Jesus came to the earth. He was born as a baby, with a physical body, God and man. In Colossians 1:15 we read that Jesus is the "exact likeness of the unseen God [the visible representation of the invisible]" (AMP). It doesn't mean Jesus looks physically exactly like God, but

---

1. "Hebrew Lexicon::H559 (KJV)." Blue Letter Bible. Accessed 27 Nov, 2013. http://www.blueletterbible.org/lang/lexicon/lexicon.cfm?Strongs=H559&t=KJV.

it means that when He was on the earth, Jesus acted the way God, the Father would have acted. We see that the Holy Spirit, the third person in the Trinity was also present at creation, "moving (hovering, brooding)" (Genesis 1:2 AMP) over the earth.

There are things about God that are hard for us to understand. For example, the Trinity, one God in three persons: how is that possible? Jesus existed before the creation of the world. At times we just need to say, God I believe the Bible although I don't completely understand how it works.

God found joy in His handiwork. He looked at creation and He said it was good. Most people enjoy creating, whether it is drawing a picture, making pottery, or building something with wood or other materials. One day I asked my son if I could throw away a clay elephant he made in art class. He answered, "No, Mom, I made that." It didn't matter whether the paint was fading and the elephant had lost part of his ear; it was special to my son, because he made it. The earth and everything God has created is special to Him, because He made it. Since He is the Creator, He takes care of His creation (Matthew 6:27-30).

Painting a Picture

When an artist finishes a beautiful painting, he steps back and looks at it. He might think, *I did a good job*, or, *this is a beautiful painting*. In the same way God created the heavens and the earth, and He looked at it and said that it was good. At the end of creation, God looked at what He had made and He was pleased with it. "And God saw everything that He had made, and behold, it was very good (suitable, pleasant) and He approved it completely" (Genesis 1:31a AMP).

There is a saying, "A picture is worth a thousand words," and I have heard people say, "You might be the only Bible someone reads," meaning that the way we behave either draws people to Jesus or pushes them away. Our actions cause people to either like us or say, "I don't want to be like that person." We are a letter being read by those around us, a letter written not with ink but by our actions, attitudes, and behavior (2 Corinthians 3:2-3).

Discovering God

Chapter 1 Discussion Questions

1. Why is it important to you to get to know God?
   _____
   _____
   _____

2. Write down what you know about God. How will you describe His character? Discuss your answers. Answers will vary.
   _____
   _____
   _____

3. Write down practical things that you can do that will help you to know God better. Make sure it will work with your schedule. Here are some ideas: Take time to read and pray thirty minutes in the morning or evening. Listen to a Bible app on your way to work.
   _____
   _____
   _____

4. God spoke the world into being; why do you think the words we speak are important? (Read Proverbs 18:21; James 3:9-10; 1 Peter 3:10.)
   _____
   _____
   _____

5. Read the passage about Paul's encounter with Jesus in Acts 9:1-7. Write down what the Holy Spirit emphasizes to you from these verses and share it with your group. Answers will vary.
   _____
   _____
   _____

> Here are some tips if the group is new to doing an exercise like this. We learn to hear God's voice and it is not difficult. In this learning process, do not be concerned about making mistakes. Just feel as you read what makes an impression on you. What phrase or words make you say, "This makes me think"? Do not be concerned whether it is your thoughts or God's thoughts. For the purpose of this exercise, just flow with the thoughts that come to your mind. If it lines up with the Bible, then write it down; if it doesn't, then move on to the next thought. We learn as we step out and do it, again and again. Because it is your personal journey, there are no wrong answers, as long as they line up with the truth of the Bible.

6. When people read the letter of your life, what do you think is the main message they will receive? Write down what you would like the message of your life to be, and an area that you need to improve in. The leader of the group can do a general prayer or divide the group in smaller groups of two to three people to pray for each other.

_____

_____

_____

> For the prayer time: Let the Holy Spirit lead you. If you sense that it is best to just close with a general prayer, then do that. If you see there are needs in the group and people could benefit from receiving prayer, then organize that in the safest way for the group, whether you put one person in the middle and the others take turns to pray for the person or divide in smaller groups. It will depend on the group and the Holy Spirit will know what is best to do. Trust Him.

Chapter 2: God, Everywhere Present in the Universe

"Thus says the Lord, "Heaven is My throne, and earth is My footstool. Where is the house that you will build Me? And where is the place of My rest?" (Isaiah 66:1)

God's Omnipresence

Where is God's house? As a child, I probably thought the church was His house or that He lived in heaven. Although heaven is a real place and we read about it in the Bible, it is not the only place where you will find God. God is omnipresent, meaning He is everywhere present in the universe. There is no place where you can go and God is not there (Psalm 139:7-10).

When you travel, you find places where a cell phone signal can't reach. I remember once how strange it felt not to be able to use my cell phone, knowing no one could call me. It made me feel isolated in some way. This young generation is called Generation C (as in Connected), because they are constantly connected to their friends through all the different electronic social media. My son recently lost his phone in the ocean on a trip. Very soon we received messages to call him on his friend's phone. He ended up not having a phone for a week and I realized how wonderful it was to be able to connect so easily with those we care about. When we talk to God, we don't even have to pick up the phone. He is always available. His communication line is never disconnected or busy.

When we talk on the telephone, the person on the other end of the line has our focused attention. God needs our focused attention too. We can talk to Him as we go along in life, but one-on-one time is needed to build a relationship. There have been times in my marriage when for a few days we were so busy that it felt like I hardly saw my husband. By the third day I would say, "I miss you, we need to find some time to talk to each other." We cannot have a relationship if we never spend time with each other or talk to each other. We also can't have a strong relationship if we are always with other people when we see each other. God is the same. He wants to have a relationship with us and if we don't take time to come to Him, He says, "I miss you." We also miss a great deal if we don't take time to develop the most important relationship we can have. We miss His counsel and direction for our lives, but above all we miss getting to know Him. No amount of time you invest in your relationship with God is wasted.

Spending time with God can be done through reading your Bible, praying, sitting in His presence, and soaking in His presence with worship music. Worship music helps me to focus my attention on God; the words help me to focus on God. I sing along or agree with my spirit as I hear, "How great is our God." When you read the Bible, be aware that many Scriptures draw us into prayer. I can pray the Word back to God as I read it. "Create in me a clean heart, O God, and renew a steadfast spirit within me" (Psalm 51:10). Yes, Lord, I ask that You will create in me a clean heart. There could be something the Holy Spirit shows you to repent about. If you feel the Holy Spirit upon a Scripture, pause and think and pray about it. Ask Him what He wants to speak to you in regard to the Scripture. Talk to God as you read the Bible. Ask Him questions or turn the Scripture into prayer.

God is everywhere present in the universe and He is everywhere at the same time. It is not that He can be everywhere present, but He is everywhere present all the time. If you really think about this statement, you will realize that no matter where you are, no matter how far away you feel from God, the truth is, He is as close as your skin all the time.

> "God is always nearer than you may imagine Him to be. God is
> so near that your thoughts are not as near as God; your breath is
> not as near as God; your very soul is not as near to you as God is.

And yet because He is God, His uncreated Being is so far above us that no thought can conceive it nor words express it."[2]

The Difference between God's Omnipresence and His Manifest Presence

God in His omnipresence fills the universe, every atom, every molecule. At times God can manifest His presence and He can be felt or experienced in some way. We read in the Bible about encounters people had with God—for example, Moses and the burning bush (Exodus 3:2). Those encounters were spectacular and life changing. The manifest presence of God is when His presence breaks through the spirit into the natural and we become aware of His presence.

Many years ago I was standing in line in a bank. Suddenly I became aware of the presence of God. I felt His presence all over me for about thirty seconds. I was surprised and astonished and I looked at the people around me, wondering if they knew what just happened. I just had an encounter with God and nobody noticed. I wondered why He did that. God has the ability to break into our lives at any time. My personal opinion about why He doesn't do that often is because He has given us free will and He desires us to live by faith. Hebrews 11 names the heroes of faith. They have one thing in common—they lived by faith.

When God meets us in an unexpected way and we become aware of His manifest presence, I receive it as a blessing or a kiss. A kiss is intimate and when God shows up in a special way in your life, you build an intimate relationship with Him. Someone once gave me a word and said that in my relationship with God He is going to wink at me. Nobody else will notice; but if I am alert, I will notice it. He wants to do that with all of us. It is those special moments when you prayed about something and you haven't seen the answer and then suddenly the answer comes, or you have been looking for a special article and find it for a special price. Involve Him in your everyday life and expect Him to show up. One time I labored hard in a task. It felt as if nobody noticed my hard work. As I was driving, I noticed a billboard on the

---

2. A. W. Tozer, *The Attributes of God, Volume 2 With Study Guide: A Journey Into the Father's Heart* (Camp Hill, PA , WingSpread Publishers, 2007), 34.

side of the road that read, "I will give you all the credit you deserve." It was an advertisement for a credit union, but I knew God was saying to me: He saw my hard work, even when no one else was noticing. That is one of those special winks or kisses. Be on the lookout to notice how He wants to meet you, even in your everyday life.

The manifest presence of God can often be felt during corporate worship. When we sing about God, Jesus, or the Holy Spirit, God reveals His pleasure and often His presence can be sensed or felt in some way. I read a book in which the writer described how he walked into a large gathering where people were worshiping and he wondered what was wrong because God's presence wasn't there. He saw the people were talking during the worship and there was no respect for God's presence. I don't enjoy talking to a person if what I say is not received or the person hardly acknowledges me or looks at me. God is the same; He looks at our hearts; and when we honor Him and focus our attention on Him in worship, He draws closer. I often feel His peace during worship. At times His presence feels like a tingly feeling. When people pray for healing, a person can feel heat or some sensation in the area where God is touching and healing them. When we praise God, honor Him, and draw close to Him, He draws near to us. When we reach out to God, He runs to meet us. He looks at our hearts more than our outward actions. The Bible tells us, "A broken and a contrite heart—these, O God, You will not despise" (Psalm 51:17b).

God's Omniscience

God knows everything that takes place on earth and in the universe. Psalm 139:1-2 describes it beautifully, "O Lord, you have examined my heart and know everything about me. You know when I sit down or stand up. You know my thoughts even when I'm far away" (NLT). Verse 4 says that He knows what we are going to say even before we say it. He knows what is going to happen to you even before you start your day. Isn't it wise to go to Him first thing and put your day in His hand? (Isaiah 55:9).

He has infinite knowledge. God has more knowledge than all the libraries in the whole world combined. In His library in heaven, we will find the secrets about how He planned and created the universe. We discover new knowledge, but He already knows it all.

I have difficulty keeping up with social media, e-mail, cell phone, and text messages. There are more than seven billion people on earth and God knows every person. He knows where they are and what they are doing. He hears every prayer that is being prayed all across the earth, without any confusion. Every cry for help is heard by Him. He knows and helps even those who don't know Him (Matthew 5:45).

How Big Is the Universe?

The earth has a circumference of 24,901.55 miles (40,075.16 kilometers). From Ohio, where I live, to Africa where I was born is a distance of more than 8,000 miles. It takes about 24 hours of air travel and layovers to get there. Within 24 hours, I can go from a country with bears, deer, coyotes, raccoons, and opossums to the grasslands of Africa with lions, leopards, hippopotamuses, rhinos, and elephants. Although it is amazing how far we can travel in a relatively short time, when we look at space the distances are hard to comprehend.

The sun is 93 million miles from earth. The speed of light is 186,282 miles per second. On average it takes sunlight about 8 minutes and 19 seconds to reach the earth. We talk about the flick of a switch. We flip a switch and the room lights up in an instant. Nothing in the universe moves faster than light.

Now let's move on to the stars. Astronomers measure stars (other than the sun) in light years. One light year is about 9.5 trillion kilometers (5.88 trillion miles). Those are distances too far for us to travel. Can you imagine—God put the stars in place, and gave them each a name? That is what Psalm 147:4; Psalms 8:3; and Psalm 147:4 tell us:

> "The moon and earth turn in such a way that we only see one side of the moon and never see the other. The eternal God is so vast, so infinite, that I can't hope to know all about God and all there is about God. But God has a manward side, just as the moon has an earthward side. Just as the moon always keeps that smiling yellow face turned earthward, so God has a side He always keeps turned manward, and that side is Jesus Christ. Jesus Christ

is God's manward face. Earth's Godward side, Jesus, is the way God sees us. He always looks down and sees us in Jesus Christ. Then we go back to the quotation from Lady Julian: 'Where Jesus appeareth the blessed Trinity is understood.'[3]

In John 14:8-9 Philip asked Jesus to show them the Father. "Philip said to Him, 'Lord, show us the Father, and it is sufficient for us.' Jesus said to him, 'Have I been with you so long, and yet you have not known Me, Philip? He who has seen Me has seen the Father; so how can you say, 'Show us the Father'?'" Jesus did not only come to die for our sins, He also came to reveal God to us, to show us what God, the Father, is like.

God's Infinitude

"Great is our Lord, and mighty in power; His understanding is infinite" (Psalm 147:5).

Words describing infinite are immeasurable, boundless, unlimited, and endless.[4] We will never find the end of God. We can travel to outer space, but we will not come to a place and find that God is not there. "'Infinite' means so much that nobody can grasp it, but reason nevertheless kneels and acknowledges that God is infinite. We mean by infinite that God knows no limits, no bounds and no end. What God is, He is without boundaries. All that God is, He is without bounds or limits."[5]

We come to the end of the road, or the end of a day, or we finish a task. We cannot comprehend how God cannot have an end or limits. "The poet says, 'One God, one Majesty. There is no God but Thee. Unbounded, unextended unity.' For a long time I wondered why he said, 'unbounded, unextended unity'; then I realized he meant that God doesn't extend into space; God contains space."[6]

How can we understand a God who contains space? If you draw a one-inch line on a paper, where the line begins represents the beginning

---
3. A. W. Tozer, *The Attributes of God, Volume 1*, 15-16.
4. *Webster's Collegiate Dictionary*, s.v., "infinite."
5. Tozer, *The Attributes of God, Volume 1*, 4.
6. Ibid., 5.

of time and where the line ends represents the end of time. Imagine that the paper is extended indefinitely in all directions. All around that line, extended into infinity in all directions around it would be God.[7] "Your throne is established from of old; You are from everlasting" (Psalm 93:2).

---

7. Tozer, *The Attributes of God, Volume 1*, 5-6.

Chapter 2 Discussion Questions

1. What does the Bible say about God and the stars in Psalm 8:3 and Psalm 147:4?

   _____
   _____
   _____

2. Read and discuss Isaiah 40:12. What do you learn from this Scripture about how big God is?

   _____
   _____
   _____

3. How big is your God? What is your view of Him? Does your view of God change when you view Him as the omnipresent, omniscient, infinite God of the universe as described in this chapter?

   _____
   _____
   _____

4. Read Psalm 139:17-18. Discuss your thoughts about this Scripture. Would it make a difference in your life if you were daily aware that God knows where you are and what you are doing?

   _____
   _____
   _____

5. Do "God's Invitation" exercise found on page 135. Use Psalm 139:1-10 for the exercise.

Chapter 3: Powerful, Majestic God

"Great is the LORD! He is most worthy of praise!
No one can measure his greatness" (Psalm 145:3 NLT).

God's Transcendence

Transcendence is not a word we hear in our everyday conversations. Transcend means to "rise above, exceed or go beyond."[8] Even though God is omnipresent, all around us, and never far from us, He is so far superior in His majesty, glory, and beauty that compared to us, He is far above us. The New King James Version of the introductory Scripture explains it well, "His greatness is unsearchable." We will go on this journey of discovering God; the excitement and discovery will never end. We can go on this journey here and now; we don't have to wait until we get to heaven.

"Christianity is a gateway into God. And then when you get into God, 'with Christ in God,' then you're on a journey into infinity, into infinitude. There is no limit and no place to stop. There isn't just one work of grace, or a second work or a third, and then that's it. There are numberless experiences and spiritual epochs and crises that can take place in your life while you are journeying out into the heart of God in Christ."[9] What a wonderful truth. When we receive Jesus, it is only the beginning of the journey with God. We miss a great deal if we don't enter in and go on this journey. Each person's journey is unique and the road map looks different. God has the map; He is waiting for you. He doesn't only have a map to help you with life decisions, He also has a treasure chest full of nuggets of truth and revelation waiting for you.

---

8. *Webster's Collegiate Dictionary*, s.v., "transcend."
9. Tozer, *The Attributes of God, Volume 1*, 3-4.

"Again, the kingdom of heaven is like treasure hidden in a field, which a man found and hid; and for joy over it he goes and sells all that he has and buys that field" (Matthew 13:44).

A few years ago as we had a prayer time for our city, I saw a treasure chest covered with dust behind a church pew. I realized that we have this treasure available to us; but if we don't spend time with God, if we don't take time to read our Bibles and spend time with Him, the treasures He has for us are like the treasures in this chest gathering dust. The Bible says God reveals Himself to the diligent seeker (Proverbs 8:17). When a dad plays hide-and-seek with his child, he will hide for a little while, but not for too long, and then he will allow his child to find him. God hides at times too, but in the process He's drawing us and giving us clues where and how we can find Him.

If I want to compare God's greatness to something on earth, the ocean comes to mind. The vastness of the ocean can be overwhelming when you sit in a boat with water all around you as far as the eye can see. A big part of my Christian journey has been like that. I just sat in the boat; I didn't know what was under the surface of the water. What I needed to do was to dive into the ocean and just like a scuba diver, explore and find out what is under the water. When we seek and run hard after God, we dive into getting to know Him and He reveals secrets to us on the journey (Jeremiah 33:3).

I had a surprising dream as I was preparing to teach about the attributes of God. In the dream I was looking at a computer screen. It had a picture of an island submerged in the ocean. The computer acted by itself and zoomed in on different areas on the island. I would see a rock, and then it would move to a plant, then a tree. On the side of the island, the ground was a bit elevated and when it zoomed to the side I saw the roots of the trees growing into the ground. Pondering this dream, I realized that studying the attributes or character of God could be compared to the computer zooming in to reveal detailed information about the island. The study reveals more detailed information about who God is. How exciting! God wants to reveal Himself to us.

We don't have to feel that we have to study much or gain a lot of knowledge. Knowledge about the Bible helps to keep us on the right path, but knowledge without a relationship with God is empty. We are on a journey focused on getting to know God and having a relationship with Him, a journey of meeting Him in the Word, meeting Him in prayer, meeting Him in the mundane routines of life. One of my sons had a very boring job last summer. I could see that it was hard for him, but I knew God was there for him—even in the challenges of the job. I told him: learn what God wants you to learn from this situation; it will not last forever. God knows where you are and what you are doing. It was good for my son to see that by the end of the summer, he had had an impact on those he worked with.

I can see my God exceeds ordinary limits. He is far surpassingly and exceedingly greater than what I can think or imagine. Isn't it wonderful to believe in a God whom you cannot limit? Often people create who God is in their own thinking. I can try to limit Him with my own thinking, but He will never fit in any box that I create. It is much better to get the right view about God from Scripture. Then we stand on a firm foundation, which cannot be shaken (Luke 6:48).

> "The transcendence of the Lord speaks of the fact that the qualities He possesses in His being and in His nature are infinitely superior to all that He has created whether in heaven or on the earth. In His being, God is infinitely higher than everything created or common. This height is in reference not to a geographical distance, but speaks of the quality of His existence, His worth that is infinite in its scope."[10]

God's Immanence

Immanent means "remaining within or internal."[11] God is not only everywhere present and all-knowing, but He also dwells in the universe. "God is omnipresent, which means God is everywhere. God is also immanent, which means that God penetrates everything. This is standard Christian doctrine, believed even in the earliest days of Judaism. God is omnipresent and immanent, penetrating everything even while He contains all things. The bucket that is sunk into the depths of the ocean is full of the ocean. The ocean is in the bucket, but also the bucket is in

---

10. Stuart Greaves, *The Existence and Majesty of God* (Kansas City, Forerunner Books, 2008), 117.
11. *Webster's Collegiate Dictionary*, s.v., "immanent."

the ocean—surrounded by it. This is the best illustration I can give of how God dwells in His universe and yet the universe dwells in God."[12]

We can at any time pray and God will hear us. His Spirit is closer than our breath. God is also working in many locations at the same time. He is actively answering prayers in the universe. His Spirit might be encouraging a person living in a persecuted country, or sending someone to pray for a sick person or help with a need. We are His hands and His feet, and one of the ways He answers prayers is through people. God's Spirit is also working in the hearts of people, preparing them to come to salvation.

> "God is immanent, which means you don't have to go distances to find God. He is in everything. He is right here. God is above all things, beneath all things, outside of all things and inside of all things. God is above, but He's not pushed up. He's beneath, but He's not pressed down. He's outside, but He's not excluded. He's inside, but He is not confined. God is above all things presiding, beneath all things sustaining, outside of all things embracing and inside of all things filling. That is the immanence of God. God doesn't travel to get anywhere. We may say in prayer, 'Oh God, come and help us,' because we mean it in a psychological way. But actually God doesn't have to 'come' to help us because *there isn't any place where God is not.*"[13]

One Saturday afternoon I felt a concern about my mother and I called her. We live in the USA and she lives in South Africa. When she answered the phone, I heard that she was not doing well. She had the stomach flu and said she was very weak. She was alone, as my brother and his family were out of town. She said she just wanted to go and lie down and hoped she would feel better the next day. All I could do was to pray. I asked God to help her, to touch her body and heal her. I prayed until I felt peace about the situation. The next morning when I called my mom she said she felt a lot better. God was there with my mom and all I needed to do was to pray and ask Him to help her.

---

12. Tozer, *The Attributes of God, Volume 1*, 137-138.
13. Ibid., 22.

What Is in a Name?

> "And they who know Your name [who have experience and acquaintance with Your mercy] will lean on and confidently put their trust in You" (Psalm 9:10a AMP).

What does it mean to know God's name? In Bible times names had meanings. *Moses* means "drawn"[14] and he was drawn or pulled out of the water. *Abraham* means "father of a multitude."[15] We can research names and find their origin and meaning. *John* means "God is gracious,"[16] *Karla* means "endearing,"[17] and *Fred* means "peaceful ruler."[18] Today people don't pay as much attention to the meaning of names.

If you hear the name of a person and you don't know the person, it is just a name like any other. If you hear the name of your best friend, the name means much more to you. The name brings back memories of good times and fun experiences. It reminds you of the character traits of your friend—that she is kind, loyal, and loves to laugh. When you know a person, there is so much more to a name.

Some of the names that the English Bibles use for God are: God, Lord, Most High God, Jehovah, and Almighty God. In Hebrew we find that the names of God are more descriptive and reveal different aspects of who God is. In Genesis 1 God reveals Himself as *Elohiym*. If I use the Hebrew meaning of God's name Genesis 1:1 will sound something like this: "In the beginning; the exceedingly great and mighty God created the heavens and the earth."[19] Another name of God is *Y@hovih, which* means, "the existing one"[20] The root word in the Hebrew connects with *Adonay* which means, "my lord, or lord of men."[21] When a person

---

14. "Hebrew Lexicon::H4872 (KJV)." Blue Letter Bible. Accessed 27 Nov, 2013. http://www.blueletterbible.org/lang/lexicon/lexicon.cfm?Strongs=H4872&t=KJV.
15. "Hebrew Lexicon::H85 (KJV)." Blue Letter Bible. Accessed 27 Nov, 2013. http://www.blueletterbible.org/lang/lexicon/lexicon.cfm?Strongs=H85&t=KJV.
16. Dorothy Astoria, *The Name Book: Over 10,000 Names—Their Meanings, Origins, and Spiritual Significance* (Ada, MI, Bethany House Publishers, 1982, 1997), 151.
17. Ibid., 56.
18. Ibid., 109.
19. Brown, Driver, Briggs and Gesenius. *The KJV Old Testament Hebrew Lexicon*, "Hebrew Lexicon entry for 'elohiym."
20. Brown, et. al., The KJV Old Testament Hebrew Lexicon, "Yahovah."
21. Ibid., "Adonay."

is called "lord" in the British society, it is a title of respect used for someone who has authority. We find the name Jehovah combined with several other names of God, *Y@hovah shammah* means, "Jehovah is there."[22] God is present in every circumstance we go through. *Y@hovah yireh* means "God sees."[23] It was first used when God provided the ram when He asked Abraham to offer Isaac. Here we see God's provision, a picture of God eventually providing His son for mankind's sin. *Y@havah shalowm* means, "Jehovah is peace." This is the name of an altar built by Gideon.[24] God revealed Himself to different people through these different names. The distinct names showed a glimpse of who He wanted to be for each situation His people were in. It is well worth the time to study the names of God. He is able to meet your need and wants to reveal Himself to you through your circumstances.

It is easier for us to picture Jesus than God, the Father or the Holy Spirit, because Jesus walked the earth and lived as a man in time and history. God we usually see as a father or grandfather type, the one who is in heaven. It is more difficult for us to picture the Holy Spirit, because we can't see a spirit. Some people think of Him as a dove, because of the word picture in Matthew 3:16, where Jesus was baptized and the Holy Spirit descended like a dove. That is just a word picture, not an actual picture of what He looks like. The baptism of Jesus is a great example of the three persons of God. "When He had been baptized, Jesus came up immediately from the water; and behold, the heavens were opened to Him, and He saw the Spirit of God descending like a dove and alighting upon Him. And suddenly a voice came from heaven, saying, 'This is My beloved Son, in whom I am well pleased'" (Matthew 3:16-17).

> "You can run through the gamut of the attributes of God and what you say about the Father you can say about the Son without modification. What you say about the Father and the Son you can say about the Spirit without modification, for there is one substance that are together to be worshiped and glorified. So when we say God is the same, we are saying that Jesus Christ is

---

22. Ibid, "Y@hovah shammah."
23. Ibid, "Y@hovah yireh."
24. Ibid, The NAS Old Testament Hebrew Lexicon, "Y@havah shalowm."

the same and the Holy Ghost is the same. All that God ever was, God still is. All that God was and is, God will ever be."[25]

---

25. Tozer, *The Attributes of God, Volume 2*, 99.

Discovering God

Chapter 3 Discussion Questions

1. Read Jeremiah 33:3. If possible read it in different translations. Write it as a prayer. Discuss in your group; what you think it means?

   _____
   _____
   _____

2. Read Revelation 21:10-25. What do you learn about the New Jerusalem, our heavenly home, from this passage?

   _____
   _____
   _____

3. When we read about God's majesty we become aware of our sinfulness. What does Hebrews 10:19-20 promise us?

   _____
   _____
   _____

4. Read Ephesians 3:19 in your own Bible and also read the Amplified Version below. What is the difference between head knowledge and what this verse refers to as "practically, through experience" to come to know the love of Christ?

   > "[That you may really come] to know [practically, through experience for yourselves] the love of Christ, which far surpasses mere knowledge [without experience]"
   > (Ephesians 3:19a AMP)

   _____
   _____
   _____
   _____

5. Discuss: How do you find treasures in the Word? Give practical advice that will be helpful to others in digging deeper into the Word.

_____
_____
_____

6. Revelation 4 is a beautiful picture of God's throne room. Do the "God's Invitation" exercise found on page 135 using this passage.

Chapter 4: Is God a Person?

"The Lord is merciful and gracious, slow to anger, and abounding in mercy" (Psalm 103:8).

God Is Spirit

Words like *Spirit* and *Holy Ghost* bring strange ideas to mind. We read in John 4:24, "God is Spirit." Add to that a God who is everywhere present and who knows everything. It is difficult for us to grasp such a big God whom we can't see. We can compare Spirit to the wind. We can't see the wind, but at times, we can feel it. We might not notice a slight breeze, but if the wind blows, we can see the leaves in the trees move and sometimes even feel the wind. Although we cannot see the wind, we know that the wind exists. God is invisible to our human eyes. There might be times when we can sense His presence, but He is not visible to our physical eyes.

What is missing in this picture is that God is a person. He is the kindest person I have ever met. We think of a person as someone who has a physical body. If I think of one of my friends, I think about their personality. To me, that is who they are. The body is not what makes us who we are. Consider this example. When we attend a viewing of a person who passed away, we see the body of the person in the coffin. We cannot have a relationship with the person anymore. If we try to talk to the person, we receive no response back. The body without the spirit and soul is just an empty shell (1 Corinthians 15:44, 1 Thessalonians 5:23). The spirit and soul forms the personality of every person we know. That is the important part of who we are. We cannot function in our earthly, physical world without a body. God created us, a spirit and a soul, living in a body.

What Is a Person?

One dictionary meaning of the word *person* is "the bodily form of a human being."[26] A person is someone who has knowledge, who can think, who has emotions and also a will to make decisions.[27]

Does God Have a Personality; Does He Feel?

We read in many places in the Bible how God felt about situations. Often He was upset with the Israelites because of their unfaithfulness. He was angry with the people when they worshiped idols, or got involved with the evil practices of the nations around them. God sent a prophet, Jonah, to turn a city from their wickedness, "Get up and go to the great city of Nineveh. Announce my judgment against it because I have seen how wicked its people are'" (Jonah 1:2 NLT). We also read about people whom He was pleased with. He said David was a man after His own heart (Acts 13:22). When we think of the central message of the gospel, "For God so loved the world" (John 3:16), it is a message of God's love. Because He loved us, He made provision to restore us to Himself.

Psalm 103 gives us a glimpse of God's personality. "The LORD is compassionate and merciful, slow to get angry and filled with unfailing love" (Psalm 103:8 NLT). We also read here that God is like a father, "tender and compassionate to those who fear him" (Psalm 103:13 NLT). We will discuss this more in a later chapter.

What Do We Learn From the Bible About God's Knowledge?

The Bible tells us that God is the Creator of the heavens and the earth. Man can create and invent—a car, a building, a computer—but we cannot create something out of nothing. We cannot create the heavens and the earth, but God did. Proverbs 1:7 tells us that, "The fear of the Lord is the beginning of knowledge." The fear of the Lord doesn't mean to be afraid of God, but it means to have respect or reverence for God and to obey Him.

---

26. *Webster's Collegiate Dictionary*, s.v., "person."
27. R. A. Torrey, *Experiencing God's Love: Understanding the Personality of God* (New Kensington, PA, Whitaker House, 1999), 11-12.

Does God Have a Will?

There are things that God decides and then there are situations where we can decide. Before Genesis 6, man lived hundreds of years. We read about the oldest man, Methuselah, who lived 969 years (Genesis 5:27). In Genesis 6:3 we read that God limited the years of a man's life to 120 years. God made the decision to limit man's life; we cannot do anything about it. We can eat healthy and exercise and that could help us to live longer, but very few people live even to 120 years.

God has given us a free will to make choices about our lives. We can choose where we live, what to wear, what to eat, or the career we want to follow. There are things that we do not have a choice about; for example, when we were born and when we will die. God's will about life and how to live a life that leads to His blessing has been given to us in the Bible.

One God, Three Persons

God reveals Himself in the Bible as one God, three Persons: God, the Father; God, the Son (Jesus); and God, the Holy Spirit. In Genesis 1:26a we read the Word *us* when God refers to Himself, "Let Us make man in Our image, according to Our likeness." Why "us," a plural word? God specifically told the Israelites that He is one God. "Hear, O Israel: The Lord our God, the Lord is one!" (Deuteronomy 6:4).

The Hebrew Word "One"

The Hebrew word translated as "one" in Deuteronomy 6:4-5 refers to a compound unity, not a simple unity. We find another example of a compound unity in Genesis 2:24, "Therefore a man shall leave his father and mother and be joined to his wife, and they shall become one flesh." The word that is used for "one God," is the same word that is translated as "one" in this passage. We can see that the man and wife are a compound unity of two—being one. Two people, uniting in marriage, come together in love, share their lives, and work together for a common goal and purpose. Differences in opinion, culture, upbringing, and beliefs can bring challenges in marriage relationships, and the couple has to come into agreement about how they are going to deal with those situations.

Our daughter is married to a wonderful American. Growing up in South Africa, we ate toast and preserves with cheese, and French toast with syrup and cheese. When my son-in-law is at our house, he shakes his head when we want to put cheese on French toast. This is not a big deal, just a cultural difference that we laugh about. In marriage a couple finds many differences that they have to deal with, some small and others more challenging to work through.

There is never a moment when God the Father, Jesus, and the Holy Spirit disagree. They are always in complete agreement, always in absolute perfect harmony and peace with each other, always enjoying each other's company. Jesus said in John 17:21, "That they all may be one, as You, Father, are in Me, and I in You; that they also may be one in Us." Jesus walked in that oneness with His Father, doing only what He saw the Father doing (John 5:19). That is what we are learning—how to live in that place of oneness and agreement with Jesus and God, through the power and work of His Holy Spirit.

A Group Can Be One

Even today we find groups of people who have the same vision and focus toward which they work. In Genesis 11:6a we see an example of a group referred to as one, "And the Lord said, 'Indeed the people are one.'" We also see this in John 17, where Jesus prayed that the church will be one, "That they may be one as We are" (John 17:11b).

God the Father, Son, and Holy Spirit have the same attributes. All three Persons of the Trinity are good, loving, kind, patient, just, holy, etc. They all have the attributes of being omnipresent, omniscient, being eternal, infinite etc. We find the Holy Spirit brooding over the earth at creation, God the Father speaking, and Jesus, being the Word, holding it all together. Then at the appointed time in history, Jesus came to earth and showed us a living example of God the Father's nature. Matthew 4:24 is a beautiful picture of God's heart where it is said of Jesus "he healed them all" (NLT). We look at a short description of each of the persons of the triune God.

God the Father

God the Father is the Creator of the heavens and the earth. He is the all-powerful, almighty, sovereign God. Jesus called Him Father and He reveals Himself as the best example of a kind, merciful, and compassionate dad who wants the best for His children. He judges sin and without a mediator, we cannot approach Him. We do not have the holiness necessary to approach God, but Jesus opened the way for us to become holy, acceptable and blameless before God (Colossians 1:22). Jesus is our mediator.

Jesus Christ, the Son of God

Jesus existed before the creation of the earth, with God, God Himself (Colossians 1:15-17). Jesus was born as a baby and walked the earth as God and man. He showed us what God is like. We read that Jesus was teaching the good news of the kingdom of heaven all through Galilee, and that He healed all sickness and disease (Matthew 4:23-24). Even after His resurrection, Jesus could be seen and touched when He appeared to His disciples (John 20:19-28).

At the appointed time, Jesus gave His life and died for our sins on a cross. He died so that we could be restored back into the relationship with God which was lost when Adam and Eve sinned. Jesus was the perfect sinless sacrifice that God required, for us to be acceptable in His sight (Hebrews 10). Jesus has a resurrected body.

We read in John 3:16: "God so loved the world." One day I read that Scripture as if I read it for the first time. I realized Jesus' death on the cross was an act of love. We do not understand that kind of love. I might be willing to lay down my life for my family or friends. Jesus willingly chose the way of suffering, and laid down His life and died on the cross for all humanity. "Greater love has no one than this, than to lay down one's life for his friends'" (John 15:13). We have the choice to receive or reject this gift.

The Holy Spirit

We read in Genesis 1 about the Holy Spirit brooding over the earth. He is omnipresent and in the Bible we read mainly about His work on earth. The Holy Spirit is God; He is a person and can be grieved (Ephesians 4:30). The Holy Spirit convicts people of sins (John 16:8). He teaches us, leads and guides us (John 14:17).

Two Scriptures that indicate that Jesus the Son is God are: John 1:1-3, 14 and John 14:7. Some examples of Scriptures that reveal that the Holy Spirit is God are: 2 Corinthians 3:17; 2 Corinthians 13:14; and 1 Peter 1:2-3.

> "The Holy Spirit is part of the Trinity. He is identified as an equal with the other persons in the Trinity (see Matthew 28:19; 2 Corinthians 13: 14). He shares with Jesus and the Father the mysterious relationship that eternally exists within the Godhead. Jesus described the kind of relationship that exists within the Trinity with statements like 'I and the Father are one' (John 10:30) 'Anyone who has seen me has seen the Father'" (John 14:9).[28]

Our bodies are a temple, a house for the Holy Spirit (1 Corinthians 6:19). In chapter 2 we asked the question, where is God's house? One answer is: in every believer who received Jesus Christ as their Savior. When we receive Jesus, His Spirit comes and dwells in us, and He is always close to us. Now that Jesus is not on earth anymore, the body of Christ is the expression of Jesus on the earth. We hear God's voice through His indwelling Spirit. Think about it. He lives in you and can speak to you or help you at any time (John 14:16).

> "A plural name was used for the one God, in spite of the intense monotheism of the Jews, because there *is* a plurality of persons in the one Godhead."[29]

The Creed of Athanasius

The Creed of Athanasius was written in the early Dark Ages and it is a very clear description of the Trinity. Below is part of the creed. It is easily found on the Internet if you would like to read the whole creed.

---

28. Robert Heidler, *Experiencing the Spirit: Developing a Living Relationship With the Holy Spirit* (Ventura, CA, Regal Books,1998), 39.
29. Torrey, *Experiencing God's Love,* 54.

Hermie Reynolds

"That we worship one God in Trinity, and Trinity
in Unity,
neither confounding the persons, nor dividing the Substance.
For there is one person of the Father, another of the Son,
and another of the Holy Ghost.
But the Godhead of the Father, of the Son, and of the Holy Ghost,
is all one,
the Glory equal, the Majesty coeternal.
Such as the Father is, such is the Son,
and such is the Holy Ghost.
The Father uncreate, the Son uncreate,
and the Holy Ghost uncreate.
The Father incomprehensible, the Son incomprehensible,
and the Holy Ghost incomprehensible.
The Father eternal, the Son eternal,
and the Holy Ghost eternal.
And yet they are not three eternals,
but one eternal.
As also there are not three incomprehensibles, nor three uncreated,
but one uncreated, and one incomprehensible.
So likewise the Father is Almighty, the Son Almighty,
and the Holy Ghost Almighty.
And yet they are not three Almighties,
but one Almighty.
So the Father is God, the Son is God,
and the Holy Ghost is God.
And yet they are not three Gods,
but one God.
So likewise the Father is Lord, the Son Lord,
and the Holy Ghost Lord.
And yet not three Lords,
but one Lord."[30]

---

30. Wikipedia contributors, "Athanasian Creed," Wikipedia, The Free Encyclopedia, http://en.wikipedia.org/w/index.php?title=Athanasian_Creed&oldid=561657811 (accessed June 28, 2013).

Discovering God

    This is a beautiful description of the unity of the three persons of God. Three in one, always in perfect unity, perfect harmony, and perfect communion. That is what He desires to bring us into, a place of rest in Him. "I have loved you even as the Father has loved me. Remain in my love" (John 15:9 NLT).

Chapter 4 Discussion Questions

1. Read Psalm 103:3-13. Write down some of the characteristics of God that are described in this passage. Share a phrase or sentence that stands out to you from this passage with your group.

   _____
   _____
   _____

2. Read the following Scriptures and find who is referred to as one?

   1 Corinthians 3:6-8: _____

   Galatians 3:28: _____

   Ephesians 4:4-6 : _____

3. Read Psalm 133:1-3. What do you learn from this Psalm about unity? What is the result of unity (see verse 3)?

   _____
   _____
   _____

4. Share practical ways with each other about how you can live John 15:9: "I have loved you even as the Father has loved me. Remain in my love" (NLT).

   _____
   _____
   _____

5. Do the "God's Invitation" exercise found on page 135 using John 15:1-10.

Chapter 5: God Is Not Limited by Time

> "The high and lofty one who lives in eternity, the Holy One, says this: 'I live in the high and holy place with those whose spirits are contrite and humble. I restore the crushed spirit of the humble and revive the courage of those with repentant hearts" (Isaiah 57:15 NLT).

God's Eternalness

Some phrases in the Bible cause me to stop in my tracks and think. Isaiah 57:15 is a phrase like that, "The High and Lofty One who inhabits eternity." If I pause and think, how long is eternity? In fairy tales people live "happily ever after." I have heard songs like "I will always love you" or "forever will I love you," meaning that the person will never stop loving another person or God, depending on who they are singing about. We sing it meaning—for a very long time, as long as I am alive, as long as I can. Forever is the longest possible time, never ending.

Eternity is described as an infinite time or duration without beginning or end. The dictionary's theological explanation for *eternity* is, "Duration without beginning or end; condition that begins at death; immortality."[31] If we see ourselves as eternal souls, living forever, then each one of us faces the question: where will I spend eternity? We can know the answer to that question. The Bible tells us Jesus is the only way to God (John 14:6, Ephesians 2:8-9, Romans 10:9).

---
31. *Webster's Collegiate Dictionary*, s.v., "eternity."

Discovering God

"Imagine for a moment that all of eternity is represented by a large piece of paper. This is where God is—unlimited by time and space. Now draw a line on that piece of paper that represents time with a beginning and an end. This line begins when God instituted time at creation, and it will end when God says, 'Time's up.'

"Man lives on the line, while God can step in and out of time according to His purposes and plans. God sees all of time at once and doesn't have to wait for anything to happen; all is *present* for Him. This is a simplified explanation of a complex idea, but it works. Because of God's position relative to time, He can—and often does—seem to answer our prayers before they have been uttered!" [32]

We cannot limit God in our understanding of time. He was not created by anyone. He never began and He will never die. He is not limited to time and space. God lives outside of time. He lives outside our sphere of life, although He is also inside it, because He is everywhere present. This is hard for us to understand, because we don't have a concept of what it would be like to exist outside of time. At times like this we can just say, God, Your ways are higher than our ways (Isaiah 55:9).

"God has no past! Now I want you to hear that. And I want you to shake your head hard here, because this is an idea that the old church fathers knew, but that we, their children, don't seem to care much about. God has no past. You have a past; it isn't really very long, although you may wish it wasn't so long. But God has no past and no future. Why doesn't God have a past or a future? Because past and future are creature words, and they have to do with time."[33]

God already knows the future. Take the example of electing a president of a country. God gives man a choice. Israel wanted a king and God gave them King Saul (1 Samuel 8:6-19). Some kings we read about in the Bible were good kings and others didn't follow and obey

---

32. Chuck D. Pierce, *Interpreting the Times: How God Intersects With Our Lives to Bring Revelation and Understanding* (Lake Mary, FL, Charisma House, 2008), 15-16.
33. Tozer, *The Attributes of God, Volume 2*, 59.

God. It's not God's fault if a king doesn't obey Him. God knows what every man will do, even before it happens. Man unfortunately has a bad track record. We haven't had many good rulers. Most people are selfish and inclined to seek their own good. God knows that. In all of this, God has a sovereign plan which will culminate in this world's ending. (In the sinful state man is in, we will never have a perfect earth.) In God's final plan, we will live with new bodies in a new heaven and earth (Revelation 21:2).

Yesterday, today, tomorrow, now, and later are all words connected to time. We live lives regulated by the clock. In the morning an alarm clock wakes us up to be in time for work. We eat at certain times of the day. Often it feels like we run a race against the clock. It feels like there is not enough time to do all the things we need to do. It is a never ending cycle. If we finish one task, we move on to the next one. In the midst of time and life changes, we have one constant and that is God. He is always the same. His character never changes. We can always depend on Him. "Lord, through all the generations you have been our home! Before the mountains were born, before you gave birth to the earth and the world, from beginning to end, you are God" (Psalm 90:1-2 NLT).

We go through times of change in our lives: changing a job or moving from one city to another, buying a house or having a child. There will always be times of change and situations that change in our lives to which we need to adapt. The Bible says Jesus Christ is the same every day—yesterday, today, and forever (Hebrews 13:8). God's character will not change. It is good to have a constant in our lives in the midst of the many changes that we go through in life.

We have a day on which we were born and a day that we will die. God has no beginning or end. God was never born and He will never die. God is not dependent on anybody. The Father, Son, and Holy Spirit are in a perfect relationship and complete unity.

How Do I Know Where I Will Spend Eternity?

The Bible records the history of God's dealings with man. God created the first couple—Adam and Eve. He made a promise that the serpent would be crushed. God chose a man—Abraham—and made promises to Him and the generations that were to come after him. The Israelites received many laws and instructions on how to live and serve God. They were a people separated unto God. There were foreigners that joined them, but those foreigners were required to follow the rules and culture of the nation of Israel.

Then Jesus Christ showed up in history. The Jewish people didn't recognize Him as the Savior God promised to them. They made even more rules than the rules God gave them, and felt that in obeying those rules they would find salvation. God made it simple. For many, it is too simple. They prefer to try and work their way into heaven or come up with their own ideas about how to get to heaven. God couldn't have made it any simpler. He made Jesus the way to Him. Jesus was the only one who could live a perfect life and be a substitute for us. I cannot live a perfect life, although I try to live a life that is pleasing to God and obey Him as best I can, I am not perfect and can never achieve perfection. Only Jesus could live a completely perfect life and be the perfect sacrifice. I simply need to accept that.

All Have Sinned

I need to admit that I have sinned. I cannot live a perfect life, a life good enough that God will allow me into heaven because of my own merit. The Bible says that we all have sinned. In fact we have a sin nature, sin in our blood, a fallen nature which comes from the blood line of Adam and Eve (Romans 5:12-18).

> "For all have sinned and fall short of the glory of God" (Romans 3:23).

Jesus Died for Us

God made provision. Even before He made Adam and Eve, He knew that in giving man free will, he would eventually make a wrong choice. Jesus is the Lamb slain even before the foundation of the world (Revelation 13:8). Jesus is the provision God made even before He created the world; He had a plan to redeem mankind, to make a way for us when we messed up.

> "For God so loved the world that He gave His only begotten Son, that whoever believes in Him should not perish but have everlasting life" (John 3:16).

Jesus told Nicodemus, who was a Jewish religious leader, in John 3:3 that he had to be born again. Nicodemus didn't understand it, but Jesus told him that there was a natural birth in which he had come into the world as a baby and then there was a spiritual birth. This is when the Holy Spirit works in our hearts and reveals the truth about Jesus Christ to us. We come to the realization we have tried to live life in our own strength; we have tried to make our own way to heaven, but we need Jesus, the one who has opened the way before us, to bring us back into relationship with God.

> "Jesus said to him, 'I am the way, the truth, and the life. No one comes to the Father except through Me'" (John 14:6).

How Do We Do This?

I need to confess to God that I need Him—confess the need of a Savior. I must ask God to forgive me of my sins and turn from sin, and receive the gift of the sacrifice of Jesus.

> "If we confess our sins, He is faithful and just to forgive us our sins and to cleanse us from all unrighteousness" (1 John 1:9).

> "If you confess with your mouth the Lord Jesus and believe in your heart that God has raised Him from the dead, you will be saved. For with the heart one believes unto righteousness, and with the mouth confession is made unto salvation" (Romans 10:9-10).

When Jesus left the earth He told the disciples that He would send the Holy Spirit who would help them (John 14:16-17). We also read that our bodies are a temple for the Holy Spirit.

> "Or do you not know that your body is the temple of the Holy Spirit *who is* in you, whom you have from God, and you are not your own?" (1 Corinthians 6:19).

When we receive Jesus as our Savior, the Holy Spirit comes and lives in our spirit. He comes and awakens us to walk in a daily relationship with God. I have heard someone said we're containers, and we leak. Daily I spend time with Jesus to be filled afresh with His Spirit, that I can become less and get out of the way, and that I can be more sensitive to His Spirit and allow His Spirit to work through me more.

Below is an example of a prayer you can pray. If you feel you can do it in your own words, then pray from your heart. Just talk to God from your heart. If you're not sure, then use the prayer.

Dear God,

I am a sinner. I cannot live a perfect life; I need help. Forgive me for the many things I have done wrong in my life. (If there are things that come to you, that you want to ask God for forgiveness for specifically, then take the time and do it.) Father God, I turn away from sin. Jesus, I receive You as the Lord of my life and as my Savior. Holy Spirit, come and fill me. Empower me to say no to sin. Thank you, God, that I am now Your child and I will live with You forever. Teach me to walk with You every day of my life. I pray this in Jesus' name. Amen.

God Created Us for Relationship

God created us to be different from the animals. Some animals learn how to do things from their parents; others don't. The Australian brush turkey builds a big compost heap for a nest. The eggs are buried beneath the compost. The parents take good care of the nest. They measure the temperature of the nest with their beaks. Just before the eggs hatch, the parents leave the nest and the young survive on their own. When the young birds are old enough to build a nest, they do it without being taught.[34]

People need to be taught. We need parents, teachers, or an adult to take care of us. We just don't know it all by instinct. God has created us to live in relationship with others. A baby is helpless for the first year

---

34. Wikipedia contributors, "Australian Brushturkey," *Wikipedia, The Free Encyclopedia*, http://en.wikipedia.org/w/index.php?title=Australian_Brushturkey&oldid=560693257 (accessed June 27, 2013).

of life; everything has to be done for the baby by someone else. Even a toddler needs many years of care and training before the child becomes an adult. When a child reaches age eighteen, they can make their own decisions. By this time, they have come to the decision whether they are going to follow the values they have been taught by their parents or whether they are choosing their own path.

God's Holiness

> "Who is like You, O Lord, among the gods? Who is like You, glorious in holiness, awesome in splendor, doing wonders?" (Exodus 15:11 AMP).

God is completely perfect, pure, and holy. Sin comes under judgment in His presence. In the Old Testament, the people had to regularly bring sacrifices for their sins. The blood of bulls and goats covered their sins for a time. They had to bring sacrifices again and again (Exodus 29:36, Hebrews 10). Leviticus 17:14 says that the life of all people and animals is in the blood. God required a blood sacrifice for the forgiveness for sins.

We read in the Bible that all people have sinned (Romans 3:23). Our sinful nature causes us to either hide from God or feel unworthy to come into His presence. People often feel that if they try harder, work harder, or do more good works to please God, they will be more acceptable to a holy God. But we miss the point if we do that. No amount of good works we do in an effort to become holy will ever be good enough to bring us into the presence of God. Only Jesus could live a perfect life and be the perfect substitute for us through His death on the cross (Hebrews 10:19). We can only receive that sacrifice; it brings such gratitude to my heart that I want to live a life pleasing to God. Receiving this grace through Jesus causes me to want to change my life, to become more like Him. I submit my life to Him and give Him permission to work in my life. What I have experienced is that He works in one area at a time. He changed my life little by little. The places where I had scars and wounds, He visited at different times and healed them all (Philippians 1:6).

> "God is not now any holier than He ever was. For He, being unchanging and unchangeable, can never become holier than He is. And He never was holier than He is, and He'll never be any

holier than now. His moral excellence implies self-existence, for He did not get His holiness from anyone nor from anywhere. He did not go off into some vast, infinitely distant realm and there absorb His holiness; He is Himself the Holiness. He is the All-Holy, the Holy One; He is holiness itself, beyond the power of thought to grasp or of word to express, beyond the power of all praise."[35]

The dictionary describes *holy* as "set apart to the service or worship of God."[36] Jesus said of the Pharisees that they cleaned the outside of the cup, but inside they were still full of greed (Matthew 23:25). Holiness comes from the inside; we receive it from God when we are washed by the blood of Jesus. It is not an outward performance. "If we confess our sins, He is faithful and just to forgive us our sins and to cleanse us from all unrighteousness" (1 John 1:9). We do not have an excuse to stay stuck in sin; we have the blood of Jesus that can cleanse us.

As Christians we can live a holy life. The idea that I am a sinner and often sin is not the right one. We should rather see ourselves as saints, who seldom sin (Ephesians 1:18). There are many Scriptures in which the Bible calls those who belong to God saints. It doesn't mean we never sin. As I walk along with the Holy Spirit, it happens that I occasionally sin. I'm not referring to major, premeditated sin. I'm referring to things like occasionally saying something that I knew I shouldn't have said. Then I have to repent or make it right. Sometimes I get offended; when this happens, there is usually an area in my life that I need to die to and lay down.

At times I have read a Scripture that told me that I wasn't lining up with God's Word, and I needed to change in an area. God does a progressive work in my life. It will start with something that happens that might be upsetting or unsettling to me. Then as I seek Him, He will bring revelation about why it is upsetting to me. Then He will show me whether I need to repent or see the situation differently. Usually it unfolds in the time period of a week or two, sometimes longer.

Learn to discipline your thought life. Sin begins on the inside, so we must discipline our minds and hearts to keep ourselves pure. Get in the habit of repenting quickly when you do something wrong. If I have any

---

35. Tozer, *The Attributes of God, Volume 1*, 160.
36. *Webster's Collegiate Dictionary*, s.v., "holy."

resentment or bitterness against a brother or sister, I deal with it right away. Keep short accounts with God and be fast to repent: that leads to the most fruitful life and a life of being at home in His presence.

The Beauty of God

People admire beauty. We love to look at beautiful nature scenes and we have admiration for a lady who is beautifully dressed. God is beautiful and that is where our desire to be beautiful originated. People pay large sums of money to try and make themselves more beautiful. The pursuit of beauty can be just an outward fleshly pursuit. There is nothing wrong with taking care of our bodies and being beautiful. The heart of the issue is that we have this desire to be beautiful, but it is not going to be satisfied by just trying to be beautiful. We will find true rest and beauty when we turn to the one who is the Creator of beauty.

When we turn our focus on God in worship and sing about how great He is, He draws us into a place of peace and holiness. When we surrender ourselves to God in worship, He draws us into His beauty and we become beautiful. My spirit has a longing for God. My spirit will never be satisfied with only seeing outward beauty; but seeing God's beauty and His holiness in the Word and in worship satisfies me deep in my spirit, and that is what I was created for. In Exodus, God manifested Himself in visible form to Moses and the elders of Israel. When we spend time in His presence, some of His glory rubs off on us and we become beautiful.

The passage in Exodus 24:9-10 describes how God met with the leaders of Israel on Mount Sinai. We read about the path that God walked on that was like sapphire stone. Stunning! It sounds similar to the picture of heaven in Revelation 4. The *Amplified Bible* says it was "a convincing manifestation of His presence." Moses and the elders ate with God. What a wonderful experience this must have been.

We can live lives of true beauty and holiness. It comes from being inwardly beautiful and having our eyes focused on God. "Give unto the Lord the glory due to His name; worship the Lord in the beauty of holiness" (Psalm 29:2).

Discovering God

Chapter 5 Discussion Questions

1. Read Romans 10:9-10 and 1 Peter 1:18-21. Do you know where you will spend eternity? Why?

   _____
   _____
   _____

2. We go through times of change in our lives. Have you experienced any changes in your life over the past year? How have they affected you? Does it help you to know that God's character doesn't change?

   _____
   _____
   _____

3. Read Isaiah 46:9-10 in different translations. Then read it below and discuss how will it help you to know that God already knows the future?

   > "For I alone am God! I am God, and there is none like me. Only I can tell you the future before it even happens. Everything I plan will come to pass, for I do whatever I wish" (Isaiah 46:9-10 NLT).

4. Read Philippians 1:6. Discuss how God works in our lives to bring change. Share an example if you have one. We encourage each other when we share what God is doing in our lives.

   _____
   _____
   _____

5. Do the "God's Invitation" exercise on page 135 using Matthew 6:19-34.

Chapter 6: All Powerful, Sovereign God

> "God has spoken once, twice I have heard this: that power belongs to God" (Psalm 62:11).

God's Omnipotence

Can you imagine how you would feel if God asked you a question? We read in Job chapters 38-41 about the many questions that God asked Job. He asked him: "Have you seen where the hail is stored? Where is the home of the east wind? Can you hold back the stars? Can you make lightning appear? Can you catch a crocodile with a hook and a line?" How would you have responded if you were Job? I know I would feel very small compared to God's power and might. Job comes out of this encounter in awe of God's greatness and majesty and he replies. "I know that you can do anything, and no one can stop you" (Job 42:2 NLT). What a revelation. This is what we need to know and be sure of. God can do anything.

One of the Scriptures in which we find the word *omnipotent* is in Revelation 19:6: "Alleluia! For the Lord God Omnipotent reigns!" Some translations use the word Almighty instead of Omnipotent. *Omnipotent* means "unlimited in ability; all-powerful; almighty."[37] God, being omnipotent, has all the might and all the power in the universe. This begs the question: if God is all powerful, why doesn't He prevent the disasters and hardships people go through? That question will be answered as we continue on this journey.

"God has power and whatever God has is without limit; therefore, God is omnipotent. God is absolute and whatever touches God

---
37. *Webster's Collegiate Dictionary*, s.v., "omnipotent."

or whatever God touches is absolute, therefore, God's power is infinite, God is Almighty." [38]

God being the all-powerful ruler of the universe deserves all the honor and glory from those He created. I watched the inauguration of an American president and it struck me how much awe and honor this man received. I thought, *God is so much more worthy of honor and often He doesn't receive it from us.* God receives such honor in heaven, but not many people on earth have the revelation of how majestic, glorious, full of splendor, and worthy of all the honor and praise God is (Revelation 5:13).

Each person has a choice to either ignore the knowledge of God, or to choose to enter into a relationship with God, through Jesus, and get to know God. We cannot see God with our physical eyes and that is why we don't see His glory as the Bible describes it. The Bible tells us in Psalm 19 that the heavens and nature declare the glory of God and it speaks without a word (Psalm 19:1-2).

Every person on earth will at some point in time be confronted with the question, "Who is Jesus to you?" The Bible says that every knee shall bow and every tongue confess that Jesus Christ is Lord (Philippians 2:10-11). It is the best choice to choose Jesus here in this life before it is too late. When Jesus asked Peter the question: "'But who do you say that I am?' Peter answered and said to Him, 'You are the Christ'" (Mark 8:29). May we have that revelation too.

People Who Walked with God

One of the most beautiful Scriptures about a person who had a relationship with God can be found in Genesis 5:24. "And Enoch walked [in habitual fellowship] with God; and he was not, for God took him [home with Him]" (AMP). How beautiful! This is my desire, to walk in habitual, continual fellowship with God. That is what Adam and Eve had. We read about the result of Enoch's relationship with God in Hebrews 11:5. Enoch was translated, or taken to heaven. He didn't die.

---

38. A. W. Tozer, *The Attributes of God, Volume 2: A Journey Into the Father's Heart* (Camp Hill, PA, WingSpread Publishers, 2007), 74.

Hermie Reynolds

Abraham's Relationship with God

We know more about Abraham than about Enoch. Abraham's dad worshiped other gods (Joshua 24:2). Abraham searched for the one true God and he found Him. God revealed Himself to Abraham. We read how Abraham left Ur to follow God. When Abraham arrived in Egypt, he didn't have faith to trust God for the safety of his wife. He was fearful for their lives and said Sarah was his sister. Sarah was taken to the king's harem. God protected Abraham and Sarah. God came to the king in a dream and told him not to touch Sarah, because she was Abraham's wife (Genesis 12:10-20). This Scripture is such a beautiful description of Abraham's relationship with God. "When Abram was ninety-nine years old, the Lord appeared to him and said, I am the Almighty God; walk *and* live habitually before Me and be perfect (blameless, wholehearted, complete)" (Genesis 17:1 AMP).

Can you imagine? The almighty sovereign God of the universe offered Abraham a relationship, to walk and live in habitual fellowship with Him. What a beautiful picture of relationship with God. We know Abraham wasn't perfect; he made mistakes. God doesn't look for perfection. He looks for a soft, humble, repentant heart, a heart that is turned toward Him. We have the same invitation; through Jesus, we can have a relationship with God, to walk with Him in a daily, moment by moment awareness of Him.

Sometimes the day can get busy and it is easy to forget to involve God in our day. Here is an idea to help you with that. Turn your thoughts to God as you go through the day. Ask Him, what are You doing in my life today? Thank Him for the many blessings you have. Ask Him to help you with your daily tasks. Develop a habit of turning your thoughts often to Him and talk to Him.

God is the source of all power. He gives power to His creation, but it doesn't mean that He loses any power. God still has all the power. On earth, our power sources can lose power. A battery runs down after a while. God is not like that. He can release power, but He still has all the power.

The Bible tells us that Jesus is all powerful too. God appointed Him "Heir and lawful Owner over all things" (Hebrews 1:2 AMP). We also learn about Jesus that "He is the sole expression of the glory of God [the Light-being, the out-raying or radiance of the divine], and He is the perfect imprint and very image of [God's] nature, upholding and maintaining and guiding and propelling the universe by His mighty word of power" (Heb. 1:3a AMP). What a powerful Scripture attesting of God's power. God spoke and everything came into being. Jesus and the Holy Spirit were partners in creating, and they are part of everything God is doing today. I am so glad I serve a God who doesn't lose His power. Forever He will be all powerful!

> "God gives power, but He doesn't give it away. When God gives power to an archangel, He still retains that power. When God the Father gives power to the Son, He keeps that power. When God pours power upon a man, He still keeps that power. God can't give anything of Himself away. God can't relinquish any of His power, because if He did, He would be less powerful than He was before. And if He were less powerful than He was before, He would not be perfect, for perfection means that He has all power. God can't 'give away' His power."[39]

> "The great God Almighty, the Lord God omnipotent, reigneth. He has now the same amount of power that He had when He made the heaven and the earth and called the stars into being. He will never have any less power than He has now, nor will He ever have any more since He has all the power there is. That is the God we serve!"[40]

God's Sovereignty

Sovereign is a word connected to a king who is the supreme ruler, the only ruler over a specific country. This king doesn't share his power or rule. He makes the decisions about everything that happens in the country. God is the sovereign, uncreated God. He is the supreme ruler of heaven and earth. When we receive Jesus as our Savior, we are transferred from the kingdom of darkness into the kingdom of light. We are spiritually transferred from Satan's rule or dominion into God's

---

39. Tozer, *The Attributes of God, Volume 2,* 75.
40. Ibid., 76.

kingdom (1 Peter 2:9). We need to remember we become citizens of a different kingdom when we give our lives to Jesus.

When we moved to the USA my visa paper read "Alien Resident." I wasn't very happy to be called an alien. The picture of a green creature supposedly from Mars came to mind. I thought about it for a day or two, and then I realized I am actually a citizen from heaven. "But you are a chosen generation, a royal priesthood, a holy nation, His own special people, that you may proclaim the praises of Him who called you out of darkness into His marvelous light" (1 Peter 2:9). Then I came to the realization that it didn't matter anymore what other people called me; I knew who my daddy was and where I belonged.

The Earth Is the Lord's

God created the earth; it belongs to Him. "The earth is the Lord's, and all its fullness, the world and those who dwell therein" (Psalm 24:1). God created the heavens and the earth. He created Adam and Eve. He is the supreme ruler of the universe. There is no one who can challenge God's power and authority.

How Do We Understand God's Sovereignty and Satan's Influence on the Earth?

Ezekiel 28 gives us some insight into who Satan is. God created him. This chapter starts off talking about the king of Tyre, but then in verse 12 it shifts and Ezekiel talks in terms that do not apply to a man. He talks about a being that was in the garden of Eden, who is covered with precious stones, ruby, topaz, diamonds and emeralds, set in gold. He was appointed a guardian angel, but then his heart was filled with pride (Ezekiel 28:13-17). The passage is talking about Satan who is behind the actions of this king. This Scripture reveals that Satan lost his position in heaven as an angel because of his pride.

God hates pride (Proverbs 6:16-17). When Satan rose up in pride, he rebelled against God and he was cast out of heaven. The pictures people draw of him are scary and dark. That is how he changed when he was banned from God's presence. We can see that he can take on the appearance of beauty. "Satan himself masquerades as an angel of light" (2 Corinthians 11:14 AMP).

How Much Power Does Satan Have?

Satan has power; we should not be mistaken about that. In Matthew 4, we read about Jesus being tempted by Satan. During the third temptation Satan offered Jesus all the kingdoms of this earth, if Jesus would only bow down before him (Matthew 4:8-9). If the kingdoms of this world didn't belong to Satan, this would not have been a temptation to Jesus. Although the earth belongs to God, Satan gained rule over earthly kingdoms in the garden of Eden. God gave Adam and Eve dominion to rule over His creation (Genesis 1:28). When Adam and Eve disobeyed God, Satan gained rule over the kingdoms of this world. When I give my life to Jesus, He brings me out of the kingdom of darkness, which is Satan's domain into God's kingdom of light (1 Peter 2:9).

> "Therefore I cannot for the life of me see any reason in the world why anyone should be fearful and timid, saying 'I'm afraid I can't make it; I'm afraid God can't keep me.' God can keep the stars in their courses and the planets in their orbits; God can keep all His vast display of might everywhere throughout His universe. Surely God can keep you!"[41]

God gave the Israelites a command in Exodus 20:3: "You shall have no other gods before Me." This is one of the Ten Commandments (Exodus 20:1-17). In the New Testament, Jesus gave one command: "So he answered and said, 'You shall love the Lord your God with all your heart, with all your soul, with all your strength, and with all your mind,' and 'your neighbor as yourself'" (Luke 10:27). As I am writing this, a song is playing about giving God first place. God is serious about this. He wants to have first place in every area of our lives. This is what it means when it says that God is a jealous God, and He is a consuming fire (James 4:5, Deuteronomy 4:24). God's desire to be first in every area of our lives means that He is relentless. He will not stop pursuing our hearts, working in our lives until we completely belong to Him. He wants you to turn wholeheartedly to Him. We might experience difficult

---

41. Tozer, *The Attributes of God, Volume 2*, 76.

circumstances that lead us to lean more upon Him. Everything He does in our lives is for the purpose that we will wholeheartedly belong to Him, that Jesus will shine through our lives.

When I was a young Christian, I thought that the longer I knew Jesus, the more I would be able to live a holy life. I didn't have the right idea, because what I was actually saying was that the longer I knew Jesus, the more I would be able to live a holy life in my own strength. What I have found as I have walked in a personal relationship with the Lord for more than twenty years is that I learned to lean much more on Jesus, instead of myself. I need His Holy Spirit's help, wisdom, and guidance in everything. What happened is He led me into a life of loving Him more, but also depending more on Him.

Discovering God

Chapter 6 Discussion Questions

1. Read Isaiah 6:1-5 and describe how Isaiah responded when He had an encounter with God.

   _____
   _____
   _____

2. Read the two Scriptures about Enoch's life below, in your Bible, and then read the Amplified version. Discuss what you learn about Enoch's relationship with God from these Scriptures.

   > "And Enoch walked [in habitual fellowship] with God; and he was not, for God took him [home with Him]" (Genesis 5:24 AMP).

   > "Because of faith Enoch was caught up and transferred to heaven, so that he did not have a glimpse of death; and he was not found, because God had translated him. For even before he was taken to heaven, he received testimony [still on record] that he had pleased and been satisfactory to God" (Hebrews 11:5 AMP).

   _____
   _____
   _____
   _____
   _____

3. Read Proverbs 6:16-19; 8:13; 11:2; 13:10; 16:18; and 29:23. What do you learn about pride from these Scriptures?

   _____
   _____
   _____

4. Pride sometimes manifests in people through criticism or the tearing down of others; it makes them feel better about themselves. Discuss what Paul says in 2 Corinthians 10:12 about comparing ourselves to others.

_____
_____
_____

5. Jesus showed us an example of humility. Use the passage in John 13:3-17 and do the "God's Invitation" exercise on page 135.

Chapter 7: God Created Me

"You saw me before I was born. Every day of my life was recorded in your book. Every moment was laid out before a single day had passed" (Psalm 139:16 NLT).

A Beautiful, Perfect Garden

Imagine living in a perfect garden, full of beautiful trees and flowers. There are all kinds of fruit to eat. Life is not hard or difficult. The fruit could just be picked and eaten with no hard work or sweat. A place where there was no sin, just joy, love, and perfect peace. It sounds like heaven!

Adam and Eve were created to live in this beautiful perfect garden. When God created the earth He made everything beautiful. For five days, God spoke and created the heavens, earth, plants, and animals. God made Adam in a different way. He took dirt and formed a man. Adam received God's personal touch. God reached down and blew His own life's breath into Adam's nose and Adam became alive, a living man, with blood flowing through His veins.

"And the Lord God formed man of the dust of the ground, and breathed into his nostrils the breath of life, and man became a living being" (Genesis 2:7). God breathed into Adam the "breath of life." "Breath" in Hebrew is the word *nĕshamah* which means, "breath of God" or "spirit."[42] "Life" is the word *chay* in Hebrew which means "living, alive, active and reviving."[43] Adam receiving the "breath of life," was receiving the breath of God or the breath of the Spirit of God, life from God which caused him to come alive.

---

42. "Hebrew Lexicon::H5397 (KJV)." Blue Letter Bible. Accessed 27 Nov, 2013. http://www.blueletterbible.org/lang/lexicon/lexicon.cfm?Strongs=H5397&t=KJV.
43. "Hebrew Lexicon::H2416 (KJV)." Blue Letter Bible. Accessed 27 Nov, 2013. http://www.blueletterbible.org/lang/lexicon/lexicon.cfm?Strongs=H2416&t=KJV.

Every person on earth has the breath of God in them, whether they know God or don't know Him. They received their life and their ability to be alive from God. "The Spirit of God has made me, and the breath of the Almighty gives me life" (Job 33:4).

Adam Was Created in the Image of God.

"So God created man in His own image; in the image of God He created him; male and female He created them" (Genesis 1:27). We know God is spirit. Jesus called Him Father. We think of Him as a grandfather type of figure. When someone encountered God in the Bible, through visions or by being taken up into heaven, we read about the glory and splendor of God as magnificent beyond words (Revelation 4 and 5). Man was created in God's image. It doesn't just refer to the outward bodily image—having hands, feet, etc. It also refers to God's character. We were created to be like Him. We read that Jesus felt compassion for the people and then He healed them (Matthew 9:36). God created us to show love to each other. He wants us to live in loving family relationships—loving those we work with and who cross our paths each day. "He has shown you, O man, what is good; and what does the Lord require of you but to do justly, to love mercy, and to walk humbly with your God?" (Micah 6:8).

How God sees us and responds to us is important. It is hard to serve God just because we must—because it's our duty to do so. If I do a job just out of duty it is much harder to do than when I do something I love. My husband loves his job and although he has many daily challenges in his work, he thrives because he enjoys his job. To serve God from a love relationship brings great satisfaction. It is much better to do right because we love someone and don't want to hurt them, than just to obey. "We love Him because He first loved us" (1 John 4:19).

We were created to bring forth the fruit of the spirit: love, joy, peace, patience, kindness, goodness, faithfulness, gentleness, and self-control (Galatians 5:22). Love wraps the package; without love all our efforts will be in vain (1 Corinthians 13:2). After Adam and Eve sinned, the works of the flesh started to manifest: hatred, fighting, jealousy, anger, complaints, criticism, etc. (Galatians 5:19-21).

People tend to judge each other by the way they look. God judges in a different way. We read in 1 Samuel 16:7 where Samuel had to anoint one of Jesse's children as the next king of Israel. God tells him, "Do not look at his appearance or at his physical stature." This is not the way God judges. "For the Lord does not see as man sees; for man looks at the outward appearance, but the Lord looks at the heart" (1 Samuel 16:7).

The Body

> "Now may the God of peace Himself sanctify you completely; and may your whole spirit, soul, and body be preserved blameless at the coming of our Lord Jesus Christ" (1 Thessalonians 5:23).

God created each person with a body, a soul, and a spirit. It is our physical flesh and blood body we have which enables us to live here on earth. Our bodies need food, which provides the energy that we need so we can work, and learn, and have fun in this life. I experience and get to know the world around me through my five senses: touch, hearing, taste, sight, and smell. God's desire for my body is that I choose to live a holy life and give my body as a living sacrifice (Romans 12:1-2). To me it means that I sacrifice every physical desire that I have that is not in line with the Word of God.

The Soul: Mind, Will, and Emotions

The Mind

The mind can be compared to a computer. What we learn and experience in life is stored in the mind. We have good experiences. We learn good beneficial habits—for example to be diligent, punctual, or hardworking. We also have bad experiences and can learn behaviors that are not according to the Bible—for example, to perceive the world with negative attitudes or to be critical. All these are stored in our minds. When we come to know Jesus, we don't receive a new computer or hard drive for our minds. Thus, my mind needs to be renewed according to the Word of God, to know how to live right (Romans 12:2).

Recently we went to the beach. I love to walk on the beach early in the mornings and see the sun rise. My husband and I were out on the beach early, only to find that it was not a great walking beach. The area where the waves were out on the shore was sloped and you had to walk with one leg three inches higher than the other leg. I was disappointed that I couldn't walk comfortably on this beach. I realized that this beach vacation was going to be different than I had expected. I had to adjust and ask God for His plan for the time I had there, instead of sulking because things didn't work out as I expected.

Will

God has given each person a will, an ability to make choices. I couldn't choose who my parents would be, but I can choose how to use the time I have been given. I make choices about the job I want to do, what I want to study, and who I want to marry. I choose daily what I want to wear and what I want to eat. We have many choices that we need to make each day. Some of those choices might not be very important; other choices have a huge impact on our lives and can affect our lives greatly. Every day, we choose to serve God through the choices we make—or we choose to serve ourselves or sin.

Emotions

We tend to see girls as more emotional; maybe they just express their emotions more freely. Men don't express their emotions as easily as women. We have three sons and a daughter. A few years ago, our one teenage son came hobbling in the front door. He didn't make a sound. I rushed to see what was wrong. His toe was bleeding; he had peeled the skin on the front of his toe. I knew that if it had been my daughter, I would have heard her from a distance. This kid didn't make a sound. Then when I tried to help him, he said, "It's not a big deal, Mom." Many boys tend to be different from girls in that way.

Men often tend to think that if they express their emotions—especially when they get hurt—it is a sign of weakness. Several years ago my husband and I went to a conference about the Father's love. God worked a great deal in our lives during that time. It was the first time I saw my husband cry. He came home and asked our kids for forgiveness; he confessed that at times he had expected them to be tough, when he needed to have compassion. God brought restoration to us and our children at that time. I learned that the important thing is not that we don't make mistakes, but that we handle them well when we do. When we make a mistake, we need to admit it and humbly repent, saying, "I'm sorry, I made a mistake." Doing this can release healing and is an honest way of walking out life. God created us with emotions. He is an emotional God. He is joyful and peaceful, and He can be happy or sad. The things that cause Him to become sad or angry are the sins of the people.

We need to learn how to deal with our emotions in a healthy way, especially when we experience negative emotions. When we are unhappy or sad, there is usually something we believe about a situation that causes us to be unhappy or sad. It helps when we change the way we think. When someone hurts us, we can take that hurt to Jesus, ask Him to help us to forgive, and ask Him to bring healing to the hurt in our hearts.

I also inherited some qualities that formed my soul. For example, my husband and I have four children: two are orderly and organized, one is more of a thinker, and the youngest one is more social. They all grew up in the same house, but they are not exactly alike. Some of the things they did, or foods they liked, were developed as a result of the culture and family they grew up in. Other aspects of their character were given by God and developed as they grew.

The Human Spirit

The human spirit is invisible, on the inside of our bodies, given by God to each person. We read in Proverbs that sorrow can impact the spirit: "A merry heart makes a cheerful countenance, but by sorrow of the heart the spirit is broken" (Proverbs 15:13). When I am awake my mind is in control; most of the time I am not aware that I have a human spirit. When I receive a message or impression from God in my spirit, it is filtered through my mind, so it feels like my own thought. Just as a small child gets to know his mother's and father's voice, we get to know God's voice as He speaks to us and we obey Him.

One morning years ago, I woke up, and still half asleep, I heard myself singing the jingle of a laundry detergent—in my mind; I thought, *what is this?* Then I woke up completely, and realized I had heard my spirit singing. I was a bit upset that my spirit was singing an advertisement from television, and I realized that I really needed to feed my spirit healthier food. Instead of watching a lot of television, I needed to listen to worship music and read my Bible more instead. Now it happens regularly that I wake up with a worship song in my mind in the morning.

Conscience

The sense of what is right and wrong is rooted in my conscience. God has given each person a conscience. God created our conscience so that we can be sensitive to what is right and wrong. We can suppress our conscience to the point where we believe things other than the Bible. My God-given conscience and the process of following and obeying the Holy Spirit work closely together (John 8:9; Acts 23:1). I have heard it explained to kids through using the example of a traffic light. When they feel peace and feel right about a situation, it is a green light. When you are not sure, it is a yellow light: wait, ask advice from a mom or dad before you do it. When you have a no feeling, it is a red light: don't do it. One time a little girl who spends one afternoon a week with me looked at the picture of a politician and said, "That guy gives me a yellow light." How wonderful if young children can learn to respond to their conscience, and how the Holy Spirit speaks to them.

God Made Man and Woman in His Image

When God created the earth, He was pleased with what He created and He said it was very good. God had joy in creating. His creation was pleasing to Him. In the center of this creation, He placed man and woman, made in His image and clothed with His glory (Genesis 1:26-27, Romans 3:23).

We were not created the same way Adam was. In Psalm 139 we read that God is very involved in our lives—even before we were born. When you know that God knew about you and that He had a plan for your life even before you were born, it will change the way you think about your life. It will give you purpose in life. You just didn't happen to be here; you are here for a purpose and God has a destiny for you.

God planned good works for each one of us to do. We were not all called to do the same thing. You are the only person who can do the good works He destined for you. "For we are His workmanship, created in Christ Jesus for good works, which God prepared beforehand that we should walk in them" (Ephesians 2:10).

Does God Love Me?

I had an eye-opening experience in my early years as a Christian. I was walking through a local bookstore. There was a stained glass ornament, with words written on it; it said something like Jesus died for me, because He loved me. I had the strangest feeling when I was looking at that. It felt as if Jesus had to do more than that to show me He loved me. It was very hard for me to receive the love of Jesus. (Later I learned that I felt like this because of the effect of my relationship with my dad in my life.) Thinking about it, I realized how ridiculous that feeling was. There was nothing greater a person could do than to die for someone. God started a process through this that exposed the wounds in my heart and led me on a path of healing.

Not long after that I read John 3:16, "For God so loved the world that He gave His only begotten Son, that whoever believes in Him should not perish but have everlasting life." Although I have heard this Scripture many times before, this time when I read it, the word "love" was highlighted to me. I thought, *God so loved the world. Jesus actually died as an act of love.* It was really because of love that He gave His life. Love is the word *agapao* in Greek. It means, "to love dearly, to be full of good will, to have a preference for."[44] That is God's feeling toward us.

> "Your enemy, the accuser, will tell you that God will love you someday when you are perfect in heaven. But the Holy Spirit is saying to you today, 'I love you even in your brokenness and weakness. You are my loving child. I was the One who kissed Adam and made Him into a living soul. My kiss upon your heart will give you the love you seek. I will not abandon you the next time you fail. I am yours for all time and for all eternity.'"[45]

---

44. "Greek Lexicon::G25 (KJV)." Blue Letter Bible. Accessed 27 Nov, 2013. http://www.blueletterbible.org/lang/lexicon/lexicon.cfm?Strongs=G25&t=KJV.
45. Brian Simmons, *Song of Songs: The Journey of the Bride* (Sevierville, TN, Insight Publishing Group, 2002), 20.

Chapter 7 Discussion Questions

1. How much money would it cost to rescue a person from hell? (Psalm 49:7-9).

2. List one reason why God should help you in a time of trouble?

3. Read Psalm 91:14 in your Bible. Then read the Amplified version below. What is the requirement in this verse to receive God's help and deliverance?

    "Because he has set his love upon Me, therefore will I deliver him; I will set him on high, because he knows and understands My name [has a personal knowledge of My mercy, love, and kindness—trusts and relies on Me, knowing I will never forsake him, no, never]" (Psalm 91:14 AMP).

4. Read Psalm 1:1-3; what is the result when a person chooses God's ways?

5. Read Romans 1:6. The Amplified version reads "Called of Jesus Christ and invited [as you are] to belong to Him." Do you feel that God accepts and loves you the way you are? If you do not feel accepted as you are, why do you feel that way?

6. Do the "God's Invitation" exercise on page 135. Use Psalm 139:13-18.

Chapter 8: God Gives Me a Choice

"And if it seems evil to you to serve the Lord, choose for yourselves this day whom you will serve, whether the gods which your fathers served that were on the other side of the River, or the gods of the Amorites, in whose land you dwell. But as for me and my house, we will serve the Lord" (Joshua 24:15).

Back in the Garden

Here we are, back in the garden of Eden. Think about it, a perfect garden—you are not afraid of any of the animals no matter how dangerous they are. It is never too hot or too cold, just the right temperature. You have no worries about what to eat or what to wear. Nobody hurts one another, and you have never heard of anyone dying or being killed. It sounds like heaven. I would definitely enjoy living in a garden like that.

"The Lord God planted a garden eastward in Eden; and there He put the man whom He had formed" (Genesis 2:8). This is where Adam and Eve lived, in this perfect garden. They didn't know evil existed; they only knew that which is good. God told them to rule over the animals. They ate fruit and seeds, and the thought of killing an animal had not even entered their minds. They had a relationship with God; He came to them in the evenings and walked and talked with them. There was only one thing that could jeopardize their perfect world, and that was their free will to make choices. God gave them only one rule to obey. That doesn't sound too difficult to do.

Free Will

A marionette is operated by a puppeteer. The puppet cannot make any decisions by itself. It just acts as the master pulls the strings. God could have created a world like that, a perfect world where He pulled all the strings and all the people (puppets) behaved exactly the way He wanted them to behave. A perfectly controlled world in which God made all the decisions for everyone He created might sound like a good idea. Nobody ever makes a mistake. My children never embarrass me. They behave perfectly all the time. My kids might say, that would be a great world—my mom would never embarrass me. Such a utopia sounds wonderful, but I know what my husband would say about that: Boring! A world like that would lack excitement; it would be dull and predictable.

Giving Adam and Eve the ability to make a choice was a risk God took. Think about it this way: I would not want my husband or my children to love me because they were told to do so. I want them to love me because they have a relationship with me and they want to love me. That is what God chose too. He gave Adam and Eve the opportunity to choose to love and obey Him. That kind of love puts us at risk though; we face the possibility of being rejected.

God took that chance. He created Adam and Eve with a free will. He gave them one command to obey. "And the Lord God commanded the man, saying, 'Of every tree of the garden you may freely eat; but of the tree of the knowledge of good and evil you shall not eat, for in the day that you eat of it you shall surely die'" (Genesis 2:16-17).

They were told not to eat from was the tree of "the knowledge of good and evil." Living in the garden before they sinned, Adam and Eve didn't have knowledge about good and evil. It is hard for us to imagine what that would be like. It might be somewhat similar to a child who easily trusts people, who is naïve and innocent. God knew Adam and Eve would not live in this perfect garden forever without disobeying Him. He knew what was going to happen even before He created the world. We read that Jesus was the Lamb slain before the foundation of the world (Revelation 13:8).

God made provision for sin even before He created the world. He chose not to create us like puppets. He created us with an ability to choose and an ability to love. Why do you think Jesus said the first commandment is, "Love the Lord your God" (Luke 10:27)? God desires our love. He wants us to make that decision with our free will, choosing to love Him. He also created us with an ability to fall in love. He is wooing us into a love relationship with Him. Not only to choose to love Him, but to really love Him with our whole hearts. The book of Hosea describes how Israel was like an unfaithful wife; it reveals God's desire that she will return to Him: "'But then I will win her back once again. I will lead her into the desert and speak tenderly to her there…When that day comes,' says the LORD, 'you will call me "my husband" instead of "my master"'" (Hosea 2:14, 16 NLT).

Two Trees in the Garden

> "And out of the ground the Lord God made every tree grow that is pleasant to the sight and good for food. The tree of life was also in the midst of the garden, and the tree of the knowledge of good and evil" (Genesis 2:9).

If we look at the words that different Bible translations use for the "tree of knowledge of good and evil," we gain greater insight into the meaning of this Scripture. The *Amplified* version reads "[the difference between] good and evil and blessing and calamity" (Genesis 2:9b AMP).

The Command God Gave Them

God told Adam and Eve that they could eat from any tree in the garden, except from the tree of the knowledge of good and evil. If they ate from that tree, they would die. God gave them this one command to obey. The perfect garden didn't last long as far as we know; no children were born in the garden. Adam and Eve ate regularly from the tree of life; the Bible tells us that eating from that tree caused them to live forever. When they sinned, they weren't permitted back into the garden; God didn't want them to eat from the tree of life and live forever in their sinful state (Genesis 3:22-23).

This was a test of obedience for Adam and Eve. Would they choose to obey God, or would they listen to another voice and decide for themselves? They decided to listen to the Serpent and follow their own desires. This is where we often get into trouble—when we trust in our own understanding and do not listen to the Holy Spirit, or when we do not know the Word of God well enough to make wise decisions.

Making Choices

Every person on earth has the ability to make choices. We make choices daily in the different situations of our lives. God is not responsible for our wrong choices. When we end up in a bad situation or get in trouble because of wrong choices, it is not God's fault. Yes, He allows people to have a free will and to do sinful things, but God is not at fault because a drunk driver kills another person in a car crash. That person made a horribly bad choice and caused harm to an innocent person. God knows that just like the Prodigal Son—when someone gets to the end of themselves, the result will most likely be a heart turning back to Him (Luke 15:11-32). It is important to make wise choices; it leads to walking in the blessing and favor of God.

The First Temptation

I remember the days of sibling fights. "He did it!" "No, he did it!" It was so hard to try and find out who really started the fight. Here in Genesis 3, we see where the blame game started. Adam blamed Eve, and Eve blamed the Serpent (Genesis 3:1-7, 10-13). We do that too; we blame our friends, brother, sister, or our parents. Blaming someone will not solve any problems. God gave us a way to deal with sin, and the quicker we deal with sin, the easier life will be. Blaming someone else just prolongs the pain. I have to deal with my sin or someone who has sinned against me; and then I need to forgive and let go of any judgments I am holding against that person. I know it is easier said than done, especially when the offense caused a lot of pain (Matthew 6:15). What I have learned is that I can ask Jesus to help me to forgive when I feel I can't forgive. It also helps to pray a blessing over the offender, not because you feel like it, but to sow into the positive and get out of the negative.

What do we do with our own sin? We ask Jesus to forgive us our sins and ask Him to cleanse us. It is good to repent specifically when the

Holy Spirit convicts us of something we did wrong. For example, it is good to say, "Forgive me, Jesus, that I was rude to so and so," instead of a vague, general prayer. If the sin was of a kind that hurt another person's feelings, I will go and ask them for forgiveness if possible. Sometimes we need to forgive ourselves for something we have done.

Many schools have zero tolerance policies toward drug abuse. That is what we need to have toward sin. If we have decided ahead of time that we are going to say no to drugs or alcohol or sexual immorality, then our mind is made up. If a person continues to struggle in these areas, then it is best to ask a pastor or leader to pray with you. There are ministries that specifically minister to people who struggle with certain areas of sin. If you are not winning the battle by yourself, get help.

There have been times where I have felt bad about something I have said, long after Jesus had forgiven me. Just as a computer has a delete button, if you have dealt with sin and made restitution (if it was necessary), then push delete, remove it from your thoughts, and continue to walk with the Holy Spirit. Receive the truth of the Word that when you confess, Jesus forgives you. "If we confess our sins, He is faithful and just to forgive us our sins and to cleanse us from all unrighteousness" (1 John 1:9).

Growing up, if we did something wrong, often our parents remained mad at us for the rest of the day, so we still felt bad for a day before we felt forgiven. This is often what we tap into when we don't feel forgiven, how we as a child felt bad for a time before we felt we were forgiven. If we have a sensitive conscience then we do feel bad when we sin and that is how it should be. The proper function of our conscience is to warn us ahead of time not to do something wrong, rather than making us feel bad afterward.

God Comes for a Visit

How would it be to walk with God in the garden? I know I would look forward to a daily visit from God, unless I had done something wrong. Adam and Eve heard the sound of God walking in the garden, which means they must have heard it before. This time they hid, because of sin; they disobeyed God's instructions. God called to Adam, "Where are you?" (Genesis 3:9).

Sin caused two reactions with Adam: fear and shame. We experience those emotions too. God called Adam; Adam said he hid because he was afraid and he was naked. Sin entered the human race through Adam and Eve (Romans 5:12). We have this tendency to sin called the sin nature. The purpose of the law (the Ten Commandments, Exodus 20:1-17) was to show us we need a Savior, that we cannot live a perfect life in our own strength. Usually we don't have to think about the Ten Commandments; we know them. God calls us into a higher level of walking with Him. He doesn't want us to just outwardly have the right behavior and do the right thing. He wants our hearts and attitudes to be right. I keep my heart pure before God and repent quickly when I get annoyed or irritated with a situation. I keep my thought life pure and discipline my thoughts when they wander into a wrong direction. This is what is described here, "I will put My laws in their mind and write them on their hearts; and I will be their God, and they shall be My people" (Hebrews 8:10b). The desire to obey Him comes from the inside—from our hearts—and it is not just outward right behavior.

Clothed in God's Glory

Let us come back to Adam and Eve. They realized they were naked. We learn from Psalm 104:1-2 how God clothes Himself. God is clothed with splendor and majesty; He wraps Himself in light. It is possible that Adam and Eve were clothed or covered with this same light or glory of God. "For all have sinned and fall short of the glory of God" (Romans 3:23). Similar words for "glory" in Romans 3:23 are splendor, brightness and magnificence.[46] Adam and Eve lost this glory-covering that God clothed them in when they sinned. Then they saw they were naked. They also lost the close relationship they had with God.

The Way Back

God made a way for us to be restored in our relationship with Him, through the blood of Jesus. Why is blood so important? In the book

---

46. "Greek Lexicon::G1391 (KJV)." Blue Letter Bible. Accessed 27 Nov, 2013. http://www.blueletterbible.org/lang/lexicon/lexicon.cfm?Strongs=G1391&t=KJV.

of Leviticus, it is written that life is in the blood. "For the life of the flesh is in the blood, and I have given it to you upon the altar to make atonement for your souls; for it is the blood that makes atonement for the soul" (Leviticus 17:11). If a person loses more than forty percent of his blood, he will not be able to stay alive.[47] *Atone* or *atonement* means "to stand as an equivalent; to make amends," "specifically the expiation of sin made by Christ."[48] God decided that blood is the only thing that can make amends for sin. Sin in the Hebrew is the word *chata'*, which means, "to sin, to miss the mark, or wander from the way."[49] In the Old Testament we read about animal sacrifices that people offered as atonement for sin (Leviticus 4). In the New Testament the word "repent" is used. The word "repent" in the Greek is the word *metanoeō* which means to change one's mind. It is not just confessing our sins, but turning away from them. [50]

Adam and Eve saw God kill an animal to make clothes for them from its skin (Genesis 3:21). What a shock it must have been to them. Up to now, they had never seen an animal killed and probably hadn't seen blood either. This could have been where God showed them that an animal sacrifice was necessary to atone for sins. We see Cain and Abel (Genesis 4: 3-5), Noah (Genesis 20:8-9), and Abraham (Genesis 15 and 17) bringing offerings or sacrifices to God. Then God gave Moses the Law and the instructions to build the tabernacle. God also gave them instructions for the worship in the tabernacle: the duties of the priests and how the offerings and sacrifices should be made (Leviticus 1-9).

For about four thousand years, animals were offered to God to atone for sin. Then Jesus was born. Jesus was crucified at the same time the Passover lamb was killed.[51] Jesus was the perfect sacrifice; no longer was it necessary to kill animals to bring sacrifices. All those offerings they made, pointed to the one final offering that would be made for all mankind. Hebrews 10 explains it well: the priests made offerings day by

---

47. Wikipedia contributors, "Bleeding," *Wikipedia, The Free Encyclopedia,* http://en.wikipedia.org/w/index.php?title=Bleeding&oldid=561475888 (accessed June 27, 2013).
48. *Webster's Collegiate Dictionary*, s.v., "atone," and "atonement."
49. "Hebrew Lexicon::H2398 (KJV)." Blue Letter Bible. Accessed 27 Nov, 2013. http://www.blueletterbible.org/lang/lexicon/lexicon.cfm?Strongs=H2398&t=KJV.
50. "Greek Lexicon::G3340 (KJV)." Blue Letter Bible. Accessed 27 Nov, 2013. http://www.blueletterbible.org/lang/lexicon/lexicon.cfm?Strongs=G3340&t=KJV.
51. *Life Application Bible*, Tyndale House Publishers, Inc. and Youth for Christ, Wheaton, Illinois, Footnote, 1968, 1971, 1986, John 19:36-37, p.1599.

day, but those offerings could never take away sins. Jesus was the only one who could take away sins. He did it by making one sacrifice for all sin, by giving His own life; and in so doing, He opened the way for us that we can stand before God as perfect and holy (Hebrews 10:11, 12 and 14).

In AD 70, the temple was destroyed and animal sacrifices stopped.[52] Jesus came; He was the perfect sacrifice and it wasn't necessary to sacrifice anymore. Hebrews 10:19-20 reveals how Jesus opened the way for us so that we can enter into God's presence with confidence, knowing that He will receive us. There is only one way we can enter and that is with our sins covered or taken away through the blood of Jesus (Colossians 1:21-22). When God looks at us through the blood of Jesus, He sees us as not guilty, blameless, pure, and holy. "Therefore, brethren, having boldness to enter the Holiest by the blood of Jesus, by a new and living way which He consecrated for us, through the veil, that is, His flesh" (Hebrews 10:19-20).

Hebrews 10:14 can be somewhat confusing. It reads, "For by one offering He has perfected forever those who are being sanctified." The word *sanctify* means "to make sacred or holy; to make free from sin; to purify."[53] We confuse sanctification with justification. Through the blood of Jesus, we are justified. I have heard the word justified explained as meaning, "just as if I have never sinned." This is what the blood of Jesus does. "Yet God, with undeserved kindness, declares that we are righteous. He did this through Christ Jesus when he freed us from the penalty for our sins" (Romans 3:24 NLT). When we ask Jesus' forgiveness for our sins, we appropriate what He has done, the work of the cross; and He washes us clean. We are justified and receive the righteousness of Jesus.

There is a difference between justification and sanctification. The blood of Jesus justifies us and we stand clean and holy before God, just as if we had never sinned. Sanctification is the process of being changed into the image of Jesus. I still have my memories and what I have learned programmed in my mind. Sanctification is how we are

---

52. Wikipedia contributors, "Repentance in Judaism," *Wikipedia, The Free Encyclopedia,* http://en.wikipedia.org/w/index.php?title=Repentance_in_Judaism&oldid=552980146 (accessed June 27, 2013).
53. *Webster's Collegiate Dictionary,* s.v., "sanctify."

being changed by the Holy Spirit; our minds are being renewed. As we walk with the Holy Spirit and we do something wrong, we repent and come back and stand as righteous and justified before God.

There have been times in my life when the Holy Spirit opened up areas in my past to bring healing—for example, in the area of my relationship with my dad. The Holy Spirit used a book to open up the hurts that I had in that area. He also showed me judgments I had against my dad. I repented of it when He revealed it. That was part of God's sanctification process in my life.

Every day we can stand righteous and justified before God, through the blood of Jesus. We just follow and obey His Holy Spirit. If there is anything He wants to deal with in our lives, He will show us. He usually works in a series of events. I might attend a meeting and something I hear there makes me think about something else. Then something else happens, and that confirms, or reveals more. Usually the Holy Spirit unfolds things over a few days until I get to the place of repentance to receive the necessary emotional healing in the area He is working in. Someone once said, "What God reveals, He also heals." I have learned that when the Holy Spirit reveals an area of hurt or a wounding in my life, it is to heal it. When it comes to the surface it is painful, but as I deal with it and repent or take it to God and ask Him to bring healing, He does. It is painful for the moment, but it is best to press through and deal with it, and allow God to bring healing.

In the years that I have been a prayer leader, I know that the one thing the enemy has tried to bring against me most is to say, you're not good enough to do this, or you're too sinful. Then I had to stand on the blood of Jesus and say I am justified and righteous through the blood of Jesus. If there is anything I need to repent of the Holy Spirit will show me, but I don't have to feel not good enough to pray or do what God has called me to do. I am qualified, because the blood of Jesus qualifies me. My ability to act and lead others cannot be based on my feelings, but on God's truth.

We have the blood of Jesus available to us; the best way to deal with sin is to deal with it quickly. Run to the cross, because eventually you will stop before you have to run to the cross and say it is not worth it. I am not going to do this anymore. I am rather going to love and obey God.

We will always and forever be thankful for what Jesus has done for us on the cross. There is no way to freedom outside of the cross. There is no way to eternity outside the cross. My son, Estian, saw a beautiful vision when he was about eleven years old. He saw a field that was all burnt down. Everything was black and burnt. Then he saw the cross and a light shining from behind the cross. In the vision, the grass started to sprout green leaves and the plants started to grow and look beautiful. That is what the cross does. Our lives can feel like everything has been wasted, like that burnt-down field, but when we go to Jesus and kneel at the cross, He gives us new life. He brings hope, growth, and goodness into our lives. Psalm 40:1-3 is a beautiful picture of this, "I waited patiently for the Lord; and He inclined to me, and heard my cry. He also brought me up out of a horrible pit, out of the miry clay, and set my feet upon a rock, and established my steps. He has put a new song in my mouth—praise to our God."

Chapter 8 Discussion Questions

1. What do you learn about the tree of life from the following Scriptures:

Genesis 3:22: _____

_____

Revelation 2:7: _____

_____

Revelation 22:2: _____

_____

2. Name some choices that you can make that won't make a big difference to the way you live your life.

_____

_____

_____

3. List a few choices that a person could make that could affect his or her life in a very negative way.

_____

_____

_____

4. Look at the choices that can affect a person negatively. How long do you think people take when they make these decisions? Which kind of decisions do you think get a person in trouble—those that are carefully considered or those that are hasty and impulsive?

_____

_____

_____

Discovering God

5. Sin caused two reactions with Adam—fear and shame. We experience those emotions too. How do we deal with it? Read 1 John 1:9 and Psalm 103:12 and discuss how you will deal with fear and shame.

_____

_____

_____

6. Read Colossians 1:21-23 in your Bible, then read the version below. Is this the way you feel in your relationship with God?

> "This includes you who were once far away from God. You were his enemies, separated from him by your evil thoughts and actions. Yet now he has reconciled you to himself through the death of Christ in his physical body. As a result, he has brought you into his own presence, and you are holy and blameless as you stand before him without a single fault. But you must continue to believe this truth and stand firmly in it. Don't drift away from the assurance you received when you heard the Good News." (Colossians 1:21-23a NLT).

7. What do you learn about justification and righteousness from Romans 5:12-19?

_____

_____

_____

8. From the Scriptures below name two benefits that the blood of Jesus gives us.

Hebrews 10:12, 14: _____

Hebrews 10:19-20: _____

Chapter 9: A Joyful, Loving, Tenderhearted, Kind Father

"The LORD is like a father to his children, tender and compassionate to those who fear him" (Psalm 103:13 NLT).

Jesus and His Relationship with His Dad

In the times that we live in, and with our busy schedules, family relationships can be challenging. We learn how to relate to other people growing up in a family. That experience will greatly shape our lives. Close relationships can be challenging. There is a saying that opposites attract, so usually when two people get married they have opposite personalities. I am more of an introvert; I need alone time to sustain the energy and strength I require to be with people. My husband is the opposite; he gets energized by being with friends. God created us all differently; family relationships were His idea. Sometimes I wonder if He doesn't chuckle when He sees two people marrying and think, "I wonder how they are going to get along." Actually He may laugh because He knows exactly how they will get along! Marriage is a picture of what Jesus did for us. When two people get married, each of them lays down their lives for the sake of the other to make it work.

In family relationships, we learn to lay down our lives too. We learn to do what Jesus did, to serve others. My mom once said she would fight like a lioness for her children, meaning that she would go to great lengths to make sure her children were safe and doing well. Being a mother myself, I have seen how blessed I am when my children flourish and grow up and make wise decisions. I have also seen how concerned I am when a child is struggling and not doing well. I have suffered through seasons of intense prayer that God would help my child to get

Discovering God

to the other side of the challenges they were facing. There is no one who will pray daily for their child like a mother will. Mothers actively show their concern for their children.

It is difficult to live in close relationship with others and not get angry or hurt at some point. If you haven't realized it already, personality clashes will surely show you we need Jesus. It is hard to get along in our own strength. "I," "me," and "my" get in the way. Jesus gave us the example before He went to the cross when He said, "Father, if it is Your will, take this cup away from Me; nevertheless not My will, but Yours, be done" (Luke 22:42).

Family relationships were God's idea. Jesus called God *Abba*, which means "My Father" or daddy. When the disciples asked Jesus to teach them to pray, Jesus taught them to pray "Our Father in heaven" (Matthew 6:9). When we know Jesus, we have the key to restoration in relationships and that is forgiveness.

Jesus called God *Abba* (Mark 14:36). *Abba* is an Aramaic word used by children to address their father, similar to the Greek word *patēr*.[54] Slaves weren't allowed to call their master *abba*. In today's terms, it would be similar to "daddy." It is a word that shows the unreasoning trust of a little child in his dad. It reminds me of how our children would jump from the side of the pool, with unwavering trust that their daddy would catch them.

Trusting God was an area with which I had a lot of trouble. It became so obvious that I had a problem in this area that I started to pray about it and seek God to reveal to me why it was so hard for me to trust Him. I was burned with boiling water when I was one year old and that opened a door to fear in my life. At the time when the Holy Spirit was bringing healing into my life around that situation, He showed me that God helped me and brought me through that situation, that I was not alone.

A few days later, He brought another incident from my childhood to mind. When I was in high school, my mom planned a vacation. One day she would say, we're going on vacation, and the next day she said there

---

54. "Greek Lexicon::G3962 (KJV)." Blue Letter Bible. Accessed 27 Nov, 2013. http://www.blueletterbible.org/lang/lexicon/lexicon.cfm?Strongs=G3962&t=KJV.

wasn't enough money, and then the following day, she was planning the vacation again. In the end we went on vacation and enjoyed it very much. As I was praying about this situation, the Holy Spirit showed me that as a child I didn't understand that my mom processed things outwardly by talking about them; this caused me to go on a roller coaster of "We're going," "No, we're not going." Subconsciously I expected God to act like my mom and change His mind frequently. That belief made it difficult for me to trust Him. I took the matter in prayer to God. I repented of any judgments that I had in that situation (Matthew 7:1-2) and God brought me to a greater level of trust. As children, we do not have the capability to look at situations objectively and that is why often in childhood, beliefs that aren't true get stuck in our minds. For example, when two parents get divorced, many children feel like it was their fault. Most of the time it wasn't, but children are too young to see situations objectively.

We don't read much about the relationship between Jesus and His earthly family. We can imagine it was similar to the traditional Jewish family, where children learned the Scriptures and learned a trade from their dad. We read that after the birth of Jesus, an angel gave Joseph (Jesus' earthly dad) a dream to flee to Egypt, when Herod decided to kill all the children younger than two. When Jesus was twelve, we read that Joseph and Mary went to Jerusalem for the Passover, and on their way home they couldn't find Jesus and finally found Him in the temple. Jesus said He was busy with His Father's business. Jesus, already at twelve years old, had had the revelation that God was His Father (Luke 2:41-52).

Learning in the Hebrew Culture

The Hebrew method of teaching differs from the way we learn in the West. Most of our learning happens in a classroom setting. In the Hebrew culture, besides reading and writing, a lot of learning comes through hands-on experience. Learning happened in everyday life, when the children went to the market with their mother to buy vegetables, when the dad was working in the field or measuring as he was building. At age thirteen, a boy would start an apprenticeship in the craft that his dad was trained in.

The rabbis (pastors or teachers) of those days had disciples or followers who lived with them, ate with them, and traveled with them. They considered learning not only head knowledge, but something learned and absorbed by spending time in the presence of the teacher. We can see it with Jesus too, who had twelve disciples who traveled with Him, and learned from Him.[55]

What to Do with the Pharisees?

The Pharisees watched Jesus closely. They tried to trick Him with questions. In Luke 14 we read that they asked Him whether it is lawful to heal on the Sabbath. Jesus answered them with a question in Luke 14:5: "Which of you, having a donkey or an ox that has fallen into a pit, will not immediately pull him out on the Sabbath day?" Jesus shows them that they who are earthly fathers and owners will have compassion for a hurt animal. How much more will God have compassion for those who are sick? God is more concerned about the sick person than about the laws of the Pharisees. When Jesus was asked what the greatest commandment was, He answered: "'You shall love the Lord your God with all your heart, with all your soul, and with all your mind.' This is the first and great commandment. And the second is like it: 'You shall love your neighbor as yourself'" (Matthew 22:37-39). Jesus revealed God's heart of compassion for people.

In Luke 15 the crowd gathered around Jesus and the Pharisees complained that Jesus welcomed sinners and ate with them (Luke 15:2). When Jesus told them that the great commandment is love, He showed them that relationship is more important to God than law. God values relationship. If we first love God and walk and live in a love relationship with Him, His love will fill us to love those around us.

In answer to the question why Jesus eats with sinners He told three parables to the crowd: the parable of the lost sheep (Luke 15:1-7), the parable of the lost coin (Luke 15:8-10) and the parable of the lost son (Luke 15:11-31). Through these parables He reveals God's pursuing heart. The first two parables are about searching: a shepherd leaves his ninety-nine sheep to search for the one who is lost and a woman who

---

55. Ann Spangler and Lois Tverberg, *Sitting at the Feet of Rabbi Jesus* (New York, HarperCollins Publishing, 2009), 51-53.

loses a coin searches for it until she finds it. Jesus' message is clear; God doesn't give up on a person. He continues to pursue those who are lost until they come to know Him.

The Parable of the Prodigal Son

In Luke 15, we find a son who asks for his inheritance while his father is still alive. Most of us would say, "I wouldn't even dare to ask such a thing." In the Middle Eastern culture, it was even more of an insult. In that culture, the son's behavior meant he wished his father was dead; and according to Jewish law, this father should have taken the son to the elders of the town and the son would have been stoned (rocks would have been thrown at him until he died).[56]

When we read this chapter, we look at it from our perspective. I have sinned; I messed up. I am like this prodigal son. When we view this parable from the father's perspective, the whole picture changes completely. This father acted counter-culturely and gave his son his inheritance although he probably knew the son would squander his money.

The Joyful, Loving, Tenderhearted, Kind, Forgiving Father (Luke 15:11-31)

"But when he was still a great way off, his father saw him and had compassion, and ran and fell on his neck and kissed him" (Luke 15:20). "The father saw him coming." This dad was on the lookout for his son's return. A father with a hard heart might say, "I never want to see that wayward son again." This is not how the father responded in this parable. The father was filled with joy; he welcomed his son and told his servants to prepare a feast. He gave him a robe and put a ring on his finger. The father valued his relationship with his son more than he valued his earthly possessions or money. This reveals God the Father's heart. No matter how badly we have messed up, He is waiting for us to come back into relationship with Him. God is a joyful, loving, tenderhearted, kind, forgiving father. He is seeking; He is looking to find the lost sheep and the lost coin; He is longing for the return of His son.

---

56. Jack Frost, *Experiencing the Father's Embrace: Finding Acceptance in the Arms of a Loving God* (Lake Mary, FL, Charisma House, 2002), 60.

Think about it. How would most fathers respond if a child wasted a lot of his money? Most fathers would be very upset and think about how hard they worked to earn all that money. The dad might think of a way to discipline the son or to make him pay him back. God as a waiting Father doesn't react like this and is not overly concerned. He just waits patiently. God is the most secure father we will ever know. He knows if a son goes astray, that when he hits rock bottom, he will return. In this parable of the prodigal son, God is this joyful, loving, tenderhearted, kind, forgiving father. This dad forgives; he has no resentment or bitterness toward his son when he returns. He is secure in his position as a father. His relationship with his son is more important to him than the money he has lost. To have his son's heart is more important to him than the squandered inheritance.

God Has Children, but No Grandchildren?

Think about this statement: God has children, but He doesn't have grandchildren? When a mom and dad adopt a child, they sign a paper in which they promise that they will take care of the child. The Bible talks about God adopting us. God adopts us into His kingdom when we receive Jesus and become His children (Ephesians 1:5, Galatians 4:5, Ephesians 5:1). God used this concept to get my attention. Pondering this statement, I realized that if my mom and dad were children of God, then I was a grandchild of God and if God doesn't have grandchildren, then who was I? I realized I needed to make a personal commitment to Jesus Christ. Attending a Bible study led by a ministry team to college students, I came under the conviction that Jesus Christ was not at the center of my life and I prayed and asked Jesus Christ to be my Lord and Savior and take first place in my life.

Even though I had given my life to Jesus, I didn't live at rest in Him. I felt like I could never do enough to please Him. I lived in fear that I would not please Him, not be good enough, or that I would mess up. I didn't feel accepted and loved by my heavenly Daddy, no matter what the Word told me. I read the Bible through a filter that I was not good enough and could not perform well enough. Now I understand that it was actually the filter I had from my earthly parents, wanting to do well for them and sometimes fearing that I was not living up to their expectations. They weren't harsh or too strict. I set very high standards for myself. I was an athlete and I was very performance oriented. I didn't know or receive the truth about what Jesus had done for me on the cross and I lived under a sense of condemnation. It was like wearing tinted glasses; I could not see God clearly because I was seeing Him through the lens of my past.

> "For you did not receive the spirit of bondage again to fear, but you received the Spirit of adoption by whom we cry out, 'Abba, Father'" (Romans 8:15).

The Difference between a Servant and a Son

What is the difference between a servant and a son? A servant works hard for his master and he earns wages. He is not a part of the family in the same way a son is. The slave leaves the master's house after he has finished his work. He has to do his job well or he will not get his wages, and he might fear that he will lose his job if the master is not pleased. The servant can only hope for a reward after serving his master well.

A son can relax in his father's house. He lives there. The son receives an inheritance; he does not earn it, and it is a gift, because he is a son. My sons love to take a nap on the couch. They can put their feet on the couch without being afraid that I will yell at them. A servant doesn't have that privilege in his master's house. He will lose his job if he has a relaxed attitude and doesn't do his job well.

A servant lives a fear-based life; a son or daughter lives at home in their father's house. "I've loved you the way my Father has loved me. Make yourselves at home in my love. If you keep my commands, you'll remain intimately at home in my love. That's what I have done—kept my Father's commands and made myself at home in His love" (John 15:9-10 MSG).

Being at home in God the Father's house cannot be separated from obedience. If my focus is to please God and honor Him, I will live at home in my Father's house. If my focus is on sin and how well I am performing, I will feel like a failure. It is better to focus on Jesus and being obedient to Him and living in His peace, focusing our thoughts upon what is good and lovely (Philippians 4:8).

Discovering God

Home is a place where I can relax. My family knows me. If they get on my nerves, I can tell them to leave me alone for a bit and they're not offended. We need a place where we can relax. Do you live as a servant or a son or daughter in your heavenly Father's house? Do you have any fear in your relationship with God? This is God's desire spoken by Jesus, "I have loved you even as the Father has loved me. Remain in my love" (John 15:9 NLT). The New King James Version reads "abide in My love." God had to set me free from being performance oriented to being able to be at home in His presence—to live in that place of perfect peace and not to be in fear that I might have done, or will do, something that will cause Him to be displeased with me.

Testimony

My earthly daddy passed away when I was sixteen years old. I never had a great relationship with my dad. He worked very hard; he wasn't home a lot; and he wasn't very involved with my life. When I entered into a relationship with my heavenly Daddy, through Jesus Christ, I tried to earn His approval. On Sundays I could feel God's presence during worship; but during the week, it felt like He was not there. God was absent just like my daddy had been. Jesus said in John 15:15, "No longer do I call you servants, for a servant does not know what his master is doing; but I have called you friends."

I didn't know how to be a friend or a daughter of God. I wasn't even aware that I was trying to earn God's approval. Subconsciously my relationship with God was fear-based and I had not yet found that place of security in what Jesus had done for me. One day I found this Scripture, "And this includes you, called of Jesus Christ and invited [as you are] to belong to Him" (Romans 1:6 AMP). I soaked in this truth. God has invited me into a relationship with Him; I belong to Him, not when I have changed or feel good enough. He loves me today even in my brokenness. He loves me and accepts me. As I learned more truth, I learned to base my faith on what Jesus had done and not on my performance—trusting God that His Holy Spirit would help me and work in my life and change me to become more like Jesus.

Church Family

Just as we grow up in a family, God has relationships with other Christians ordained for us that will help us grow in Him. It is hard to stay alive in our faith and passionate for Jesus if we do not have fellowship with other Christians. The church is described as having Jesus as the head and those who believe in Him as the body. We all fit in somewhere in the body of Christ (Ephesians 5:23, Hebrews 10:25). Think about it like this: If you take a coal out of the fire, the coal won't burn very long. The coal needs to be together with the other coals to keep on burning. We encourage each other when we spend time together in the Word and in praying together. "And they steadfastly persevered, devoting themselves constantly to the instruction and fellowship of the apostles, to the breaking of bread [including the Lord's Supper] and prayers" (Acts 2:42 AMP).

Chapter 9 Discussion Questions

1. God needs to be first in our lives, followed by our family and other relationships. Do you value relationships more than being the best in your work or what you pursue in life?

   _____
   _____

2. What is the view that you have of God? Do you believe He is compassionate and wants to help people? Take some time to ponder and find out what you really believe about God. (If it does not agree with the view we've discussed here, it is good that He brings that to the surface. He wants to reveal Himself to you and show you who He really is.)

   _____
   _____

> Questions 3-6 could expose areas of fear, problems with trust, or rejection issues. If the group leader feels that the group would benefit from a time of prayer about the issues that surfaced in the group, then go ahead and do that; otherwise move on to Question 7.

3. Do you live as a servant, or a son or daughter in your heavenly Father's house?

   _____
   _____

4. Do you have fear in your relationship with God?

   _____
   _____

5. Answer this question: I believe God loves me, because…

_____
_____
_____

> Discern what you believe in your heart. Sometimes I believe something different in my heart than what I believe in my mind. If you answer the above question truthfully, it will show you what you really believe.

6. Read Proverbs 3:1-14. Do the "God's Invitation" exercise on page 135 using this passage.

Chapter 10: God Keeps His Promises

"For I the Lord your God am a jealous God, visiting the iniquity of the fathers upon the children to the third and fourth generation of those who hate Me, but showing mercy and steadfast love to a thousand generations of those who love Me and keep My commandments" (Exodus 20:5b-6 AMP).

Tricked into a Covenant?

When the Israelites entered the Promised Land—Canaan—God told them not to make any covenants with the nations in that area. Not long after entering Canaan, they came across a traveling group. The people of Gibeon had put on old clothes and carried torn wineskins to give the impression that they had traveled a long way from a far distant country (Joshua 9). Joshua believed them and was tricked into making a covenant with them. Even though the Israelites were tricked into this covenant, they did not break the covenant. They considered making a covenant serious business, and they didn't go back on the promises of the covenant they had made.

People made agreements or contracts from the earliest times in history. They called them covenants. Nations made covenants to help each other during times of war. A covenant today would be like a business contract or a marriage; it is legally binding. Usually both parties benefit from the covenant. In the Bible, we read of covenants that God made with man. We find two types of covenants in the Old Testament. One type is between two parties who have something they can share; they both bring something to the covenant. The other type is when one person has everything to give and the other person has nothing to contribute, but simply receives the benefits. This is the kind of covenant that God makes with us. He gives and we receive.[57]

The Covenant between God and Noah (Genesis 6-9)

As we read the Bible, we see how God looked for a person or a group of people with whom to make a covenant. He looked for someone who was searching for Him and wanted to worship Him. As part of the covenant, God made promises to people. During Noah's time, God looked at the earth and saw that the people were evil. We see God's heart in Genesis 6:5: "The LORD observed the extent of human wickedness on the earth, and he saw that everything they thought or imagined was consistently and totally evil" (NLT).

God looked at the people on earth and found only one righteous man, Noah. "But Noah found favor with the LORD...Noah was a righteous man, the only blameless person living on earth at the time, and he walked in close fellowship with God" (Genesis 6:8-9 NLT). God gave Noah instructions to build a large boat, which took 120 years to build. That is a long time to be obedient to God and to keep on obeying and following Him.

The time finally came when God told Noah and his family to go into the ark and to bring the animals into the ark. It rained for forty days and nights, and the whole earth was under water (Genesis 7). The water finally receded and dry ground appeared. Noah came out of the ark; he offered a sacrifice to God and God established a covenant with him. God promised that the earth would not be destroyed by a flood again, and He gave the rainbow as a sign of this promise (Genesis 9:11-13).

What Constitutes a Covenant?

A covenant was incomplete without the terms of the covenant—the conditions and promises that both parties should fulfill—and the oath of the covenant. An oath makes the covenant irrevocable.[58] In Exodus 2:23-25 we read that God remembered His covenant with the Israelites.

---

57. Kevin J. Conner and Ken Malmin, *The Covenants* (Portland, OR, Bible Temple Publishing, 1983), 2-3.
58. Ibid., 5.

God remembers a covenant, and acts upon it. In the New Testament, we are told not to make a vow or an oath, but to just say "yes," when we can do it, or "no" when we can't do it; to do more than that is from the evil one (Matthew 5:37). God is the only one who can keep His promises. Jesus stepped in our place and died on the cross, that we can come into a covenant with God.

When we ask God to forgive us our sins and receive Jesus as our Savior, we step into a covenant relationship with God. The covenant we are in is one in which God gives everything and we simply receive. We have nothing to offer, except our lives. In this covenant, God says, you become My child and I will take care of you. I will protect you and be with you all the days of your life. If you obey and follow Me, you will be My friend. I will bless you and My favor will be upon your life. I will share secrets from heaven with you, and you can partner with Me and pray, and see Me move, and do miracles as My kingdom comes to earth. We say, I have nothing to bring to this covenant, but myself. Father, I receive the sacrifice of Jesus on my behalf. I surrender my life to You, God. I receive Your Holy Spirit to help me live in obedience to You.

God's Covenant with Abraham

God made a covenant with Abraham, who was the first patriarch and father of the nation of Israel. Abraham believed God and his faith saved him (Galatians 3:6). We are saved through our belief in Jesus Christ (Romans 10:9-10). This covenant is wonderful; even though the promises in the Bible were originally given to the nation of Israel, they are also ours. We can take them as promises to ourselves, because of what is written in Galatians 3:29: "And if you are Christ's, then you are Abraham's seed, and heirs according to the promise." Although the Bible chronicles the history of the Israelites, through whom God fulfilled the promise made to Adam and Eve that someone coming from their generational line (Jesus) would crush the serpent (Genesis 3:15).

The Holy Spirit can breathe upon Scripture and speak to us personally. We should check our motives. If something is an idol in our lives, we can read things into Scripture that God is not saying. In everything, we need to keep our hearts pure, asking for God's will in every situation. He is not a cookie-cutter God. He has a personal plan for each person.

Discovering God

In 1999, we moved to the USA. We had four children between the ages of four and eleven, and we had to start building a new life in a new country. We used the money we had to buy furniture, a car, and the basic things we needed. At first, we lived in an apartment. As we looked at the price of houses, we realized we didn't have enough money for a down payment. We had owned a home for the twelve years that we lived in South Africa, and expected that we would be able to buy one in the United States. This was very discouraging to me; I wondered if we had heard from God correctly or not. Here we were with our four children in a small apartment! As I was praying about this and reading my Bible, I read this Scripture: "Each of you will invite your neighbor to sit with you peacefully under your own grapevine and fig tree" (Zechariah 3:10b NLT). I realized God was giving me a promise, that although it looked impossible in the natural to own a home, somehow He would make a way for us to eventually buy one. A year and a half later we were able to buy a house.

In making a covenant, two of the steps were that the covenant partners exchanged robes and also exchanged weapons.[59] God doesn't have a physical robe or weapons that He gave to Abraham. He said to Abraham, "Do not be afraid, Abram. I am your shield, your exceedingly great reward" (Genesis 15:1b). God was saying to Abraham that He would fight his battles, He would protect him. God was giving Abraham Himself when He said, "I am…your exceedingly great reward." When we step into the covenant with God through Jesus, Jesus offers us Himself (John 3:16). We exchange our sinful self for a life in Christ. "I have been crucified with Christ; it is no longer I who live, but Christ lives in me; and the life which I now live in the flesh I live by faith in the Son of God, who loved me and gave Himself for me" (Galatians 2:20). There was no better exchange than to give my life, which I selfishly lived for myself, to Jesus and allow Him to live through me instead. He knows so much better than I do what is best for my life.

When God and Abraham made a covenant, God told him to take a heifer, a ram, a turtledove, and a pigeon and split them down the middle. The only time animals were cut down the middle was when they made

---

59. Dr. Richard Booker, *The Miracle of the Scarlet Thread: Revealing the Power of the Blood of Jesus From Genesis to Revelation* (Shippensburg, PA, Destiny Image Publishers, 2008), 36.

a covenant, so Abraham knew God was making a covenant with him. Abraham fell into a sleep while the covenant was being made. When two people made a covenant in those days, they stood back-to-back between the two halves of the split animal. Then they walked around the carcasses in a figure eight and ended facing each other.[60] We read that a "smoking oven and a burning torch" moved between the animals (Genesis 15:17). Abraham couldn't be an equal partner for God in a covenant so God came and made a covenant with Himself. Abraham saw a manifestation of God—the smoking pot and burning torch—making the covenant in Abraham's place with God.[61]

The Mosaic Covenant

God brought the Israelites out of Egypt and made a covenant with them at Mt. Sinai. He gave Moses the Ten Commandments and the Law concerning the people (Exodus 19-40). We read that the Law was only a trainer or tutor to bring Israel to Christ (Galatians 3:24). The Law teaches us how to live correctly; but with the indwelling Holy Spirit, we do not need the constant reminder of the Law. We desire to live right, to obey God, and follow His Holy Spirit (Hebrews 10:16).

At the end of the forty years in the desert, God made a covenant with the new generation that would enter the Promised Land. Deuteronomy 27-33 laid out the conditions and promises for them about entering and keeping the land under their occupation.

The Palestinian Covenant

This covenant was made with the nation of Israel, "especially the second (and new) generation at the end of the forty years of wanderings in the wilderness and before they entered Canaan, the land promised in the Abrahamic Covenant. It laid out the conditions for entering into and maintaining the Promised Land"[62] (Deuteronomy 27-33).

---

60. Booker, *The Miracle of the Scarlet Thread*, 37.
61. Ibid., 61-65.
62. Kevin Conner & Ken Malmin, *The Covenants* (Portland, OR, Bible Temple Publishing, 1983), 10.

God's Covenant with David

God made a covenant with David after the death of King Saul to establish the kingdom of Israel under David. God made promises to David, that his kingdom would be established forever; and that through David's generational line, Jesus would be born (2 Samuel 7; Psalm 89; Psalm 132).[63]

David's Covenant with Jonathan

David was a shepherd; he watched his father's sheep in the field. He took food to his brothers on the battlefield and saw the giant Goliath. David, even though he was young, knew his God and couldn't let this giant insult the army of Israel. David had faith that the Lord who saved him from the bear and lion while he watched his father's sheep would help him to kill this giant. He took his slingshot and rocks and killed the giant Goliath who was mocking Israel (1 Samuel 17). This event made David famous in Israel, but David's fame and the praise people gave him caused King Saul to become jealous of him. David and Saul's son, Jonathan, were good friends and they made a covenant (2 Samuel 4:4). Jonathan helped David to escape from Saul. Later Jonathan and Saul were killed in battle, and David became king. Usually a new king killed all the relatives of the previous king, to prevent them from rising up against him and to taking the throne back. Jonathan had a five-year-old son when he was killed. Mephibosheth's nurse was afraid that the new king, David, would kill him and ran and hid at Lodebar with the boy. David responded different from other kings.

King David remembered the covenant he had made with Jonathan. He asked around to find out if there were any of Saul's relatives left. He wanted to be kind to them, because of his covenant with Jonathan (2 Samuel 9:1). This is the result of covenant. David remembered the covenant and when he found Jonathan's son, Mephibosheth, he brought him to the palace. David told Mephibosheth that he would show kindness to him for the sake of Jonathan. David restored to him the land his grandfather, Saul, had and Mephibosheth ate at David's table (2 Samuel 9:7). The children of the covenant had the option to choose whether

---

63. Ibid., 10.

they wanted to receive the benefits of the covenant. Mephibosheth had to choose to receive the benefits of the covenant his father made with David.[64] God made provision for us to become His children too. Jesus died for us to pay the price needed to come into that covenant. We, too, have the choice whether we will receive through faith what Jesus has done or reject what He has provided for us. Just as Mephibosheth did nothing to deserve this gift, we cannot earn the gift of salvation; we can just receive what Jesus has done. "But God demonstrates His own love toward us, in that while we were still sinners, Christ died for us" (Romans 5:8).

The New Covenant

The Bible talks about an old covenant and a new covenant. The old covenant operated in the Old Testament. The Israelites received the Law that they had to obey. The sign that a person had entered into the old covenant was circumcision. God told the two kingdoms—Israel and Judah—that He would make a new covenant with them (Jeremiah 31:31, Hebrews 8, Matthew 26). Jesus brought us into the new covenant. During the Passover meal with the disciples just before He was captured and was crucified, He said, "For this is My blood of the new covenant, which is shed for many for the remission of sins" (Matthew 26:28). The old covenant didn't bring people into freedom. It was in operation until Jesus died. "When God speaks of a new [covenant or agreement], He makes the first one obsolete (out of use). And what is obsolete (out of use and annulled because of age) is ripe for disappearance and to be dispensed with altogether" (Hebrews 8:13 AMP).

Jesus didn't come to abolish the law, but to fulfill it (Matthew 5:17). He fulfilled it by living the Law, and obeying it perfectly in our place. We could not do it; Jesus did it. The new covenant brings us into a different focus. We are not focused on obeying the Law of Moses, but we're focused on loving God. Because of our love and thankfulness for His grace, we love our neighbors and those who don't know Him. The focus of the new covenant is love and not law. When we act with the love of Jesus, we will obey His commandments as well (John 15:10).

---

64. Booker, *The Miracle of the Scarlet Thread*, 42-47.

Under the new covenant, we give our lives to Jesus. Baptism is a sign that we die to our old life and live in His resurrected life (Romans 6:4). The first covenant had a temple where God dwelt in the Holy of Holies and where the ark of the covenant was kept (Exodus 40). In the new covenant, the Holy Spirit comes and dwells in us. Our bodies are His temple (1 Corinthians 6:19). How amazing to think that the King of the Universe, God Almighty, does not desire a temple built with human hands; instead He desires to dwell in human hearts.

Chapter 10 Discussion Questions

1. Read Exodus 34:7. How many generations are affected by the blessings, and how many generations will sin affect?

2. Read Genesis 15:1-6 and write down the promises God gave to Abraham.

3. The old covenant had the Law. What did Jesus mean when He said He didn't come to abolish the law but to fulfill it (Matthew 5:17)?

4. What does the Bible teach about promises? Should I make promises to people? (Read Matthew 5:34-37.)

5. Should we make promises to God? (James 4:13-15)

6. Read Numbers 23:19 and 2 Corinthians 1:20. Do you think God keeps His promises?

_____
_____
_____

7. Use Hebrews 10:10-20 and do the "God's Invitation" exercise on page 135.

Chapter 11: God Is Light and There Is No Darkness in Him

"God is light and in him is no darkness at all"
(1 John 1:5b).

God Is Light

Have you ever tried to find a light switch in a dark room? If you have an idea where it is, then it is not too hard to feel your way and find it, but if you have no idea where it is, the task is quite impossible. As soon as you find the light switch and flip it, instantly light floods the room. On the first day, God created light on earth. "Then God said, 'Let there be light'; and there was light" (Genesis 1:3). God divided the light and darkness into day and night. Light travels approximately 186,282 miles per second. Natural light travels very fast. God's light, His presence, doesn't have to travel. He is omnipresent—everywhere present in the universe. His light is everywhere, even in darkness, although we don't see His light with our natural eyes. The Bible tells us that we cannot go to any place and God is not there. We can never get away from His Spirit (Psalm 139:7,12).

We also know from the Bible that God dwells in unapproachable light. I have heard testimonies of people who came back to life after they had a near death experience and many of them saw a bright light. "The King of kings and Lord of lords, who alone has immortality, dwelling in unapproachable light, whom no man has seen or can see" (1 Timothy 6:15-16). From Psalm 104:2, we learn that God is wrapped or clothed in light. I think that glory wrap was the clothings Adam and Eve wore in the garden. Can you imagine being clothed with God's presence, wrapped in His presence? Jesus walked in that kind of favor and presence of God. He had favor with God and with people (Luke 2:52).

The Bible (God's Word) Is a Light to Our Path

A few years ago I was driving down a country road at night. The moon was dim and I was surprised to see how dark it was. Then I realized what a big difference streetlights made to provide light on the road. It is the same with the lights of a car; it would be dangerous to drive at night with no lights. Just as a light helps us to see where we should drive, the Bible gives us direction for our lives, "Your word is a lamp to my feet and a light to my path" (Psalm 119:105).

The Word also brings joy to our hearts and direction to our lives. This is the result that following the Holy Spirit and obeying the Word of God will have in our lives, "The instructions of the LORD are perfect, reviving the soul. The decrees of the LORD are trustworthy, making wise the simple. The commandments of the LORD are right, bringing joy to the heart. The commands of the LORD are clear, giving insight for living. Reverence for the LORD is pure, lasting forever. The laws of the LORD are true; each one is fair. They are more desirable than gold, even the finest gold. They are sweeter than honey, even honey dripping from the comb. They are a warning to your servant, a great reward for those who obey them" (Psalm 19:7-11 NLT).

Jesus Is the Light of the World

Jesus said that He is the light of the world. "I am the light of the world. If you follow me, you won't have to walk in darkness, because you will have the light that leads to life" (John 8:12 NLT). This living Light is His Holy Spirit who brings wisdom and revelation in situations and breathes life upon Scripture. I have also experienced the Holy Spirit guiding me one step at a time. He lights up our path for the next step we have to take, but most of the time we don't see the whole picture.

Even when He brings correction through the Word, His purpose is that we will line up with the Word and be helped. Most of the time I have experienced gentle correction—drawing me in the right direction. Matthew 7:1-2 in the Amplified Bible says, "*Do not* judge and criticize and condemn others, so that you may not be judged and criticized and condemned yourselves. For just as you judge and criticize and condemn others, you will be judged and criticized and condemned, and in accordance with the measure you [use to] deal out to others, it will be dealt out again to you."

I was still a young Christian at the time when I read that verse. Over the next few days, the Holy Spirit showed me three incidents in which I had been very judgmental in my heart toward others. Although I didn't voice it and didn't say anything to anyone, God wanted me to have a pure heart and not judge by what I saw. He knew every person's heart I had judged and He knew why they acted the way they did. He wanted me to have His perspective. I repented of my judgments and asked God to forgive me and cleanse my heart. I asked Him to help me to see situations from His perspective.

When we allow the Holy Spirit to teach us, He is kind and does not bring us under condemnation. He brings conviction that allows us to change. He draws us in the right direction and He doesn't just make us feel bad about sin. He draws us to the solution, to repentance, so we can receive God's forgiveness and change the way we think or do things.

When Paul had the encounter with Jesus on the road to Damascus, Jesus told him He would send him to the Gentiles (people who were not Jews) to open their eyes and turn them from darkness and the power of Satan to God's light (Acts 26:17-18). This Scripture also tells us how He would accomplish this. The people would receive forgiveness of their sins and an inheritance among those who believe in Jesus. Isn't this a beautiful picture of the grace of God? There are no qualifications or stipulations that say that some sins are too big to forgive. He can turn anyone from darkness to light and give them a spiritual inheritance. I believe that our inheritance is to live a life that is a blessing to others, one that fits in with the good works He has planned for us to do (Psalm 16:6, Ephesians 2:10).

The Enemy Works in Darkness

> "For the enemy has persecuted my soul; he has crushed my life to the ground; he has made me dwell in darkness, like those who have long been dead" (Psalm 143:3).

The work of the enemy is often compared to darkness. "And have no fellowship with the unfruitful works of darkness, but rather expose them" (Ephesians 5:11). If we look at the difference between the fruit of the spirit: "love, joy, peace, longsuffering, kindness, goodness, faithfulness, gentleness, self-control" (Galatians 5:22-23) and the fruit of the flesh: "adultery, fornication, uncleanness, lewdness, idolatry, sorcery, hatred, contentions, jealousies, outbursts of wrath, selfish ambitions, dissensions, heresies, envy, murders, drunkenness" (Galatians 5:19-21), we can see that they are as different as day and night.

There are several reasons that we need to spend time with Jesus, reading our Bibles and praying. The first reason is to build a relationship with Him. Picture yourself taking time to drink a cup of coffee or having a meal with a friend. Those are some of the best times to talk. If you don't spend time with a friend, you don't get to know the person. It is the same with God.

We also need the wisdom of the Word. There are so many voices saying things that are contrary to the Word of God that we need to keep the Scripture regularly in front of us. There are Bible apps for smartphones and other mobile phones, and they can be helpful to listen to the Bible when driving, since many of us spend a lot of time driving.

Sometimes I feel that I need to spend more time in the presence of God. Daily we pick up stress and cares as we go through life. If we don't take time somewhere in our schedule to release those things to God, we are going to carry them ourselves and be weighed down by them. "Casting the whole of your care [all your anxieties, all your worries, all your concerns, once and for all] on Him, for He cares for you affectionately and cares about you watchfully" (1 Peter 5:7 AMP). Jesus said His yoke is easy and His burden is light (Matthew 11:30).

Walking in the Light

I have found that God is not only interested in us acting the right way. He wants us to think right too. This is why the Bible says we should meditate day and night on His law (Joshua 1:8, Psalm 1:2). Sin starts with a thought and eventually becomes an action. Philippians 4:8 tells us what we should think about, "Finally, brethren, whatever things are true, whatever things are noble, whatever things are just, whatever things are pure, whatever things are lovely, whatever things are of good report, if there is any virtue and if there is anything praiseworthy—meditate on these things." Imagine your thoughts being heard loudly and clearly in heaven. This consideration should make you quickly turn your thoughts in the right direction when they wander in a wrong direction.

Revelation from the Word

When the Israelites built the tabernacle, there was no natural light in the Holy Place. They had a huge candlestick, which could hold seven candles that provided light. In this room was a table with loaves of bread on it. The bread represents the Word of God and the candlestick, the Holy Spirit who brings light and reveals the Word to us. In the Holy of Holies where the ark of the covenant was kept, there was no natural light; the presence of God was the light.

Jesus walked in the full measure of the Holy Spirit. Isaiah 11:2 is a description of the Holy Spirit upon Jesus, "The Spirit of the Lord shall rest upon Him, the Spirit of wisdom and understanding, the Spirit of counsel and might, the Spirit of knowledge and of the fear of the Lord." Jesus had the right word at the right time for every person He encountered. When I need God's wisdom or counsel in a situation, I pray about it and I ask Him for revelation about the situation. It is much better if the Holy Spirit comes and shows me what is going on in a situation than to rely on my own wisdom.

In 1997 when we felt God was bringing a change of direction in our lives, we started to pray and seek God about it. My husband received a Scripture; and I saw a vision of our family going on a new path. It took two years before what God spoke to us was actually walked out in the natural. We moved from South Africa to the United States. Many things needed to happen. The paperwork for the visas needed to come through. We needed to sell our house and sell or give away all our furniture. In each step, we had to pray and seek God about what we should do. That took about nine months. God showed Himself faithful every step of the way. At times it felt like the transition was taking too long. I wondered, *God, why don't You move faster*, but He knew what He was doing.

We Are a Light for Jesus

> "But '*he who glories, let him glory in the Lord*'"
> (2 Corinthians 10:17).

Jesus said He is the light of the world. Then in Matthew 5:14-16 He continues that we are light to the world and that we should not hide our light under a basket, but that we need to be a light to those around us, through the good things we do that will bring glory to God. Think about it this way—Jesus has no hands or feet on earth other than those who follow and obey Him. Jesus left the earth and gave us His Holy Spirit to help us and to lead and guide us. We are His hands and feet to show His love and who He is to other people.

Every person on earth will either be drawn closer to Jesus or pushed away from Jesus depending on the experience they have with a Christian. Think—do your actions draw people closer to Jesus or push them away from Jesus? Even if a person is not open to hearing anything about Jesus, we can show the love of Jesus and silently pray for that person.

Jesus also said that the righteous will shine like the sun (Matthew 13:43). A lighthouse is a beautiful example of a light than can be seen from a distance. The light of the lighthouse shows passing ships when they are close to cliffs or rocks, or any hazardous areas in fog or at night. It guides them through the storm. A lighthouse doesn't have furniture in it, because an empty room makes the light shine brighter. To me this speaks of a life empty of self. "I have been crucified with Christ; it is no longer I who live, but Christ lives in me" (Galatians 2:20a).

Being a light for Jesus is not something we can do in our own strength. At a time in my life when I was seeking for the meaning in life, God answered my questions by giving me two Scriptures, "And this is the secret: Christ lives in you. This gives you assurance of sharing his glory" (Colossians 1:27 NLT), and "So you also are complete through your union with Christ" (Colossians 2:10a NLT). That focused my life and helped me to know that whether it is a season of abundance or a season of challenge, Jesus was enough for me, and that I should look to Him in everything. I also realized how much He had done in my life. To Him belonged the glory of all He had done and is doing in my life. "We now have this light shining in our hearts, but we ourselves are like fragile clay jars containing this great treasure. This makes it clear that our great power is from God, not from ourselves" (2 Corinthians 4:7 NLT).

God Shines His Light on Our Path Through His Spirit

God can speak to us in many different ways. He speaks to us from the Bible and through the people who daily cross our path. We read about many instances in the Bible where He spoke to people through dreams or visions. As a young Christian I read the following verse. "The LORD says, 'I will guide you along the best pathway for your life. I will advise you and watch over you. Do not be like a senseless horse or mule that needs a bit and bridle to keep it under control'" (Psalm 32:8-9 NLT). Reading this I told God that I did not want to live a life in which He continually needed to discipline me to bring me back on the right road. I wanted to live a life in which I heard His voice and obeyed Him instead.

Discovering God

Chapter 11 Discussion Questions

1. What do the following Scriptures tell you about light? Luke 2:32 (read verses 2:25-32); John 12:46 (read verses 44-46).

   _____
   _____
   _____

2. Do you think we can know the future or have an idea of what is coming or what is going to happen? Read 1 Thessalonians 5:1-5 and 1 Corinthians 2: 9-16. Discuss.

   _____
   _____
   _____

3. What do you learn about the enemy from Psalm 143:3 and John 10:10?

   _____
   _____
   _____

4. What do you learn from the following Scriptures: Psalm 119:18; Psalm 119:130; and Ephesians 1:17-19 about God's light and His Word?

   _____
   _____
   _____

5. Read Philippians 4:8 and John 8:32. When you experience negative thoughts about a situation, ask God to help you to think differently. Take some time to ask the Holy Spirit to show you if there is a challenging situation in your life that He wants you to think differently about.

6. Read Numbers 6:24-26. This is a beautiful Scripture of blessing. Write the Scripture in your own words and take some time to pray prayers of blessing over each other.

_____
_____
_____

Chapter 12: God Is Love

"He who does not love does not know God, for God is love" (1 John 4:8).

God Is Good

When I listen to the news, most of it is bad news—about crimes, accidents, hurricanes, and tornadoes. The news doesn't give me a picture of the goodness of God. It portrays a picture of a sinful world. Too much bad news can be very depressing; I need to hear good news too. We need to look beyond the daily news to find out what God is doing. In 2011 there was an uprising in Egypt and it caused a lot of turmoil and eventually a governmental change. At the beginning of that time, I heard a word from a ministry that God had plans for an awakening in the Middle East. This helped me to pray when everything seemed very dark in Egypt.

A few years ago, I took a class about Revelation, the last book in the Bible. It can be quite a disturbing book when we read its descriptions; it sounds like many people will die at that time. Then I was reminded of an incident. In 1999, half of the country of Mozambique flooded. I remember hearing on the news about a woman who gave birth sitting in a tree during that flood. Mozambique was a very challenging country for the gospel to take root. Missionaries had little success there up to that time. After the flood, breakthrough came and many new churches were planted in Mozambique and the surrounding area. I look at the disaster that happened. In God's sovereign will, He didn't intervene and stop the rain. He allowed these storms to happen and the hardened hearts of many people were opened to receive Jesus. God is most concerned that people will spend eternity with Him and get to know Him (1 Timothy 2:4). This is His priority.

> "We must not think of God as composed of parts working harmoniously. We must think of God as one. Because God is one, God's attributes never quarrel with each other. Because man is not unitary but made, because he is composed, the man may be frustrated. He may have schizophrenia, and part of him may war with another part of him. His sense of justice may war with his sense of mercy. The judge sits on a bench many a time and is caught between mercy and justice and doesn't know which to exercise…God has no parts anymore than a diamond has parts. God is all one God, and everything that God does harmonizes with everything else that God does perfectly because there are no parts to get out of joint and no attributes to face each other and fight it out. All God's attributes are one, and together."[65]

It is very important that we know that God is good. God cannot be evil. He is holy, He is just, and He judges sin. We cannot separate God's goodness and His justice; they are not contradictory. They are all part of who God is. The Bible is God's story of His dealings with man. We read of many times the Israelites disobeyed God and it resulted in them being taken captive to a foreign nation. Sin has consequences. God is slow to get angry and He is kind. He gives a chance and another chance and often many more chances than we deserve. In the last few years, there have been several words about coming disasters. Some see it as God's judgment.

If I don't know God's character when somebody blames Him for something that happened, I will doubt His goodness. He knows when each person will be born and when they will die. We live in a sinful world with a lot of evil and disease. No matter what happens, we can run to God. I have had instances where God warned me or a friend about something bad that the enemy planned for one of my kids, and prayer averted it. I have learned to press in to Him for answers, for revelation. He wants to reveal things to us. He doesn't just want us to go through one bad circumstance after the other. If you press in to Him, ask

---

65. Tozer, *The Attributes of God, Volume 1*, 65.

Him, keep on asking, pressing in, listening, watching, He will bring the answers. Some of my answers came in the form of a book I read; some came through a friend, or the TV, or a message I heard.

One day I read the book of Jonah and I realized how God gives second chances. God in His mercy sent Jonah to Nineveh to give the people an opportunity to turn from their sins. "Then God saw their works, that they turned from their evil way; and God relented from the disaster that He had said He would bring upon them, and He did not do it" (Jonah 3:10). The Living Bible reads God "abandoned His plan to destroy them, and didn't carry it through." God can change His mind when people turn from their sinful ways (2 Chronicles 7:14). When you read about accounts of revival in history, the results have been empty jails and much greater church attendance. People's lives were changed.

We cannot view God through the lens of our humanity, because He is not like us. We were created in His image and His likeness (Genesis 1:27). We do not have many of God's attributes: being omnipresent, omniscient, being infinite, not limited by time, etc. God has given each one of us an eternal soul. He has given us the ability to make choices and He has given us the ability to love. It is much better to be filled with His love and pour it out on those around us than to just try and love people in our own strength. There are times that we choose to love, but I love it when He fills my heart with His love, when I spend time in His presence in worship and prayer, and I cannot help but love those around me.

God Is Love

> "Beloved, let us love one another, for love is of God;
> and everyone who loves is born of God and knows
> God" (1 John 4:7).

One of the most well-known chapters in the Bible about love is 1 Corinthians 13. Here we read some of the characteristics of love. Love is patient and kind. The first thing I learn about love makes me realize that I can't love in my own strength. Our patience will be tested in many situations in life. If your patience isn't tested at work, it will surely be tested when you have kids. Love is never envious; it does not seek its own advantage. This is a picture of humility, of putting others first.

Discovering God

I heard a speaker say that every challenge we face is an opportunity to find out who God wants to be for us in that situation. This is a great attitude. Rather than focusing on the problem, turn the focus to God and engage Him about the situation.

> "God is one. Not only is there only one God, but that one God is unitary, one with Himself, indivisible. And the mercy of God is simply God being merciful. And the justice of God is simply God being just. And the love of God is simply God being compassionate. It's not something that runs out of God—*it's something God is!*"[66]

God Is Merciful

> "Oh, give thanks to the Lord, for He is good! For His mercy endures forever" (1 Chronicles 16:34).

The word "mercy" brings the picture to my mind of a criminal who has committed a crime and is pleading for mercy. We are in the same situation when we consider our sins. The Bible tells us that all have sinned; there is not one who is not guilty (Romans 3:23). We stand before the Judge of the universe; Satan is accusing us of sinning. God is asking, "How do you plead? Guilty or not guilty?" The beauty of the cross is that when we are asked that question, the right answer is, "I plead the blood of Jesus." Jesus died for me that I can be declared not guilty before God.

It is good to know that God doesn't want people to die without Him. He takes no pleasure in people dying without Him and living through eternity without Him. This Scripture describes God's heart toward the wicked: "Say to them: 'As I live,' says the Lord God, 'I have no pleasure in the death of the wicked, but that the wicked turn from his way and live'" (Ezekiel 33:11a). God has forever settled it in heaven that Jesus is the only way we can receive atonement for sins. Jesus is the only way to be restored into a relationship with God. God will never change His mind about it. We are the ones who need to receive the gift, the work Jesus had done for us (John 3:16). The joy that the gift of salvation

---
66. Tozer, *The Attributes of God, Volume 1,* 72.

brings to our hearts stirs our hearts to share it with others, that they can receive that gift too.

When my son, Morgan, was five years old, we would play checkers. At times I just wanted to finish the game, because I had things to do, so I deliberately made mistakes. He would stop and say, "Mommy, I will give you some mercy; I don't think you should move there. Try again." He had great mercy and compassion for his mother's mistakes.

The Difference between Mercy and Grace

Mercy and grace are the flip sides of the same coin. I have heard it explained this way: God in His mercy doesn't give us what we deserve. We deserve death, because of sin, but through, Jesus, God forgives us. *Mercy* is defined as "compassionate treatment of an offender or adversary."[67]

Grace is the "exercise of love, kindness, mercy, or favor."[68] We deserve death, but because Jesus took our place, God gives us eternal life. Grace is God's unmerited favor, His goodwill or forgiveness extended to a person.

God's Grace Opens the Way for Us to Believe in Jesus

> "For by grace you have been saved through faith, and that not of yourselves; it is the gift of God, not of works, lest anyone should boast" (Ephesians 2:8-9).

It is good to remember that we were saved by grace. In many religions, people try to do things to please their god. Even in Christianity, people sometimes have the view that if they just live a good enough life or do good works, then they will go to heaven. The Bible puts salvation and good works in a different perspective. We can do nothing to add or take away from the work Jesus has already done for us on the cross. We do good to others and live a good life because we are forever thankful for what He has done for us.

---

67. *Webster's Collegiate Dictionary*, s.v., "mercy."
68. *Ibid,* "grace."

Christmas Time

For a child the highlight of Christmas is opening presents under the tree. Usually the excitement runs high and they can hardly sleep because they are so excited to open their presents. It is unthinkable that someone would just walk by the Christmas tree and say, "Oh, there is a nice present for me under the tree," and not open the present, but just continue with life as usual instead.

That is what many people do with Jesus. Jesus is the ultimate gift that God has given us. When Jesus talked to the woman at the well in John 4:10, He answered her and said, "If you knew the gift of God." Our eyes need to be opened to realize the gift we have been offered. It is a free gift. Some people hear about Jesus, but then decide to ignore the gift. We receive God's gift. That is what we mean when we say that we are saved by grace. Personally each one of us needs to say yes to Jesus, and receive Him as our Savior. We must ask God to forgive us our sins and turn from sin.

We receive salvation by grace. Good works are the outlet and the overflow of the grace we have received. I am so thankful that God saved me that I want to help others and I want to do God's will. Good works are the overflow of my love and relationship with Jesus. They are the evidence of my salvation (James 2:17).

God's Empowering Grace

We read this about Jesus as a child, "And the Child grew and became strong in spirit, filled with wisdom; and the grace of God was upon Him" (Luke 2:40). What did that look like? Numbers 6:24-25a comes to mind, "May the LORD bless you and protect you. May the LORD smile on you" (NLT). It must have been something like this: God's blessing, His favor; His joy was upon, over, and around Jesus' life, continually blessing Him and protecting Him wherever He went. Then we read in Acts 4:33 that the apostles witnessed with great power and that great grace was upon them all.

As I learn more about God's grace, I ask for more of His grace when I go through a difficult time. We live in times in which we need great grace to be strong in our faith and walk with God. There are many distractions and activities that try to draw us away from God. Our spiritual eyes need to be open to recognize these things; and we need God's great grace to be a blessing to those around us. The Bible tells us that the fear of the Lord is the beginning of wisdom (Proverbs 9:10). I think walking in God's favor and the fear of the Lord are connected: having respect and reverence for God, and living in obedience to His Word. "The fear of the Lord leads to life, and he who has it will abide in satisfaction; he will not be visited with evil" (Proverbs 19:23).

God's Grace Enables Us in Our Weakness

> "And He said to me, 'My grace is sufficient for you, for My strength is made perfect in weakness.' Therefore most gladly I will rather boast in my infirmities, that the power of Christ may rest upon me" (2 Corinthians 12:9).

Paul talks about a thorn in the flesh; some translations refer to this as an infirmity or a hardship that Paul had to endure. To me this weakness reminds me of those areas that we are not naturally strong in. Nobody has a 100 percent perfect personality—to be always accurate, on time, friendly, kind, and gracious. In the areas in which I am not naturally strong, God's help is available for those weaknesses. When we first got married, John procrastinated a lot when he had to fill out any paperwork. He would do the taxes at the last minute. I do things earlier rather than late, so it tested my patience greatly. I complained; I nagged; and I saw that it did not help at all. I struggled with occasional depression, but as I searched for answers, God set me free. Over the years the Holy Spirit has brought much change in John and in my life, especially in going to Him with those areas where we need help in. I have learned to ask for God's help often and to ask for His grace. I need it.

God Is Compassionate

> "Now it happened in the process of time that the king of Egypt died. Then the children of Israel groaned because of the bondage, and they cried out; and their cry came up to God because of the bondage. So God heard their groaning, and God remembered His covenant with Abraham, with Isaac, and with Jacob. And God looked

upon the children of Israel, and God acknowledged them" (Exodus 2:23-25).

Jesus often showed compassion for people and healed them (Mark 6:34). When God actively had compassion on His people, He did four things: He heard their groaning; He remembered His covenant; He looked upon their sufferings and pitied them; and He came and helped them. At times we pray and it feels like God is not answering the prayer. There comes a time when God hears and He answers.

This is just the beginning of your journey with God. He has many surprises waiting for you. He is set to win your heart. He has one goal in mind—to win your love for eternity. I am very grateful that He has called us into a love relationship with His Son. Jesus is the Bridegroom King who will return for us (Revelation 19:6-9). The Holy Spirit is preparing us for Him. He is making us pure and holy, changing us day by day. Even though we can look forward to spending eternity with God, it doesn't start there. It starts here and now in our everyday relationships and the work that we do. God is here with us now. He wants to lead us into the blessing of living with Him here and now, knowing His presence and seeing His work in our lives, living in His peace. "I have loved you even as the Father has loved me. Remain in my love" (John 15:9 NLT).

Chapter 12 Discussion Questions

1. Daily we hear a lot of negative news. Read each of the Scriptures below twice. The purpose of this exercise is to try and discern how these Scriptures make you feel, compared to how you feel when you listen to the news. Discuss how the Word and the news affect you differently. See Psalm 34:8; Psalm 119:68; and Psalm 139:16-18.

_____

_____

_____

2. Do you think the following statement is true? "The strength of my Christian walk will depend on the revelation that I have of who God is." Discuss this.

_____

_____

_____

3. Jonah ran away from God and found himself in the belly of a whale. Desperate situations cause people to turn to God. Read how Jonah responded in Jonah 2:1-10. Discuss the changes that you see in this from the time Jonah ran away to what he is saying in this prayer.

_____

_____

_____

4. What is the progression in Matthew 22:37-39? Discuss why this order is important. What would happen if we flipped the progression?

_____

_____

_____

5. Read 2 Corinthians 12:9 in your Bible. Then read it in the *Amplified* version (printed below). What does this Scripture mean to you personally?

> "My grace (My favor and loving-kindness and mercy) is enough for you [sufficient against any danger and enables you to bear trouble manfully]; for My strength and power are made perfect (fulfilled and completed) and show themselves most effective in [your] weakness. Therefore, I will all the more gladly glory in my weakness and infirmities, that the strength and power of Christ (the Messiah) may rest (yes, may pitch a tent over and dwell) upon me!" (2 Corinthians 12:9 AMP).

_____
_____
_____

6. Do the "God's Invitation" exercise from page 135 using 1 John 4:7-21.

God's Invitation

This is an exercise to give God an opportunity to speak to you. The boundaries for this exercise are:

- Confidentiality: If someone shares a personal issue that God is speaking to them about, it stays in the group.

- No counseling: This not a time for counseling or the giving of advice. It is a time for every person to seek God to hear from Him personally.

- This is not a time to focus on the history of a Scripture verse or content, unless the Holy Spirit wants to speak to you about it. *The focus of the exercise is to hear God's voice about a personal situation in our lives.*

- Remember we are all practicing. Don't stress out! Don't try to figure out whether it is your thoughts or God's thoughts. His voice sounds the same as our thoughts, and the longer you walk with Him the more you will be able to discern His voice. If you're just beginning this journey, go with the thoughts that come to you first, unless they don't agree with the Bible. If you're not sure about a thought, just wait a little bit longer and see what God says about it. If I am hearing from God, I will sometimes say, "I take my thoughts captive unto the obedience of Jesus Christ," especially if I feel I am thinking too many random and distracting thoughts (2 Corinthians 10:4-5).

Structure:

1. One person reads the Scripture passage.

2. Each person should spend 15-30 minutes listening to the Holy Spirit and journaling. (How long you choose to spend on this depends on the group.) You can have worship music playing softly in the background. Find the word or phrase that the Holy Spirit wants you to focus on and ask God this question: What is Your invitation to me with this Word or Scripture? Journal the thoughts that come to you.

3. At the end give each person an opportunity to share what the Holy Spirit is speaking to them personally.

4. Once everyone has shared, the leader may close with prayer. He can decide if he wants to ask if anyone has a specific need for prayer and take time to pray for that, or to just take prayer requests to be prayed for during the week.

About the Author

Hermie Reynolds and her husband, John, live in Hamilton, Ohio, and have four grown children. She taught in a public school until she had children, and then she and her husband led the children's ministry in their church in South Africa for ten years. In 1999, they moved to Cincinnati, Ohio. She has since taught many classes about the attributes of God, and prayed for the Cincinnati region for more than ten years, at the Cincinnati House of Prayer. John and Hermie are part of the Oxford Vineyard Church planting team.

www.ingramcontent.com/pod-product-compliance
Lightning Source LLC
Chambersburg PA
CBHW050540300426
44113CB00012B/2202